Connecting
with the
PAST

Connecting
with the
PAST

History Workshop in Middle and High Schools

CYNTHIA STOKES BROWN

HEINEMANN
Portsmouth, New Hampshire

Heinemann
A division of Reed Elsevier Inc.
361 Hanover Street
Portsmouth, NH 03801-3912
Offices and agents throughout the world

Every effort has been made to contact the copyright holders for permission to reprint borrowed material. We regret any oversights that may have occurred and would be happy to rectify them in future printings of this work.

The author and publisher wish to thank the children and parents who have given permission to include material in this book as well as those who granted permission to reprint previously published material:

Excerpts from "Examining Historical Roots of Racism and Anti-Semitism," Part I, by Allen Stoskopf, from *Facing History and Ourselves News*, Fall 1991, reprinted by permission of the author.

Library of Congress Cataloging-in Publication Data

Brown, Cynthia Stokes.
   Connecting with the past : history workshop in middle and high
schools / Cynthia Stokes Brown.
     p. cm.
   Includes bibliographical references (p.).
   ISBN 0-435-08901-3 (acid-free paper)
   1. History—Study and teaching (Secondary)—United States.
I. Title.
D16.3.B78 1994
907'.1'273—dc20
                                       94-15077
                                          CIP

Editor: Toby Gordon
Production: Nancy Sheridan
Cover design: Darci Mehall

Printed in the United States of America on acid-free paper
2000   EB Digital   4   5

Contents

Preface

Five years ago I received a letter from Karen Jorgensen asking whether I would like to collaborate with her on a book about teaching history. I knew at once I would say "yes." I deeply respected Karen's published curriculum on immigration, New Faces of Liberty (Zellerbach Family Fund, 1988, grades 5–8), and we enjoyed working together on its sequel, New Faces in Our Schools: Student Generated Solutions to Ethnic Conflict (Zellerbach Family Fund, 1992, grades 9–12). Since Karen is an experienced elementary teacher and I teach prospective secondary teachers, we thought that by writing together about how young people learn history we could cover the whole range of schooling from kindergarten through high school.

For several years we met for Sunday morning talks and exchanged drafts of tentative chapters. We started by discussing the relationship of history to language arts, and within months we arrived at the term history workshop to name our constellation of ideas. Eventually teaching history K–12 proved too much for one book, and we each settled for our end of the continuum. Heinemann brought out Karen's book in 1993, History Workshop: Reconstructing the Past with Elementary Students. I am deeply indebted to Karen for developing the ideas with me, for pushing me hard in the direction of trusting students, for support and challenge every step of the way. My debt to her will be clear to readers of Connecting With the Past.

For my love of history and teaching I am indebted to a long line of people, including my paternal grandmother, Francis Fountaine Stokes, who taught in a one-room school in Elkhorn, Wisconsin, and my maternal grandparents, Bertha and Jacob Bast, who hosted family summer camp for all the city cousins and children on their dairy farm near Milwaukee, Wisconsin. My mother, Louise Bast Stokes, provided the most important reading for my adolescence when she bought a set of Harvard Classics with her first paycheck in the early 1930s. She and my father, Stanley Thomas Stokes, love young people and have modeled teaching in many ways throughout their lives. My high-school boyfriend, Horace Cox, filled me with tales of bygone days and family genealogies, and my seventh-grade teacher, Edith Sammons, set us to investigating our hometown, Madisonville, Kentucky. Two outstanding teachers at Duke University, Harold Parker and I.B. Holley, Jr., showed me what history could be. Dr. Parker confided that he kept his seven different plans for teaching freshman history in his safe deposit box at the bank, which taught me to attach the proper value to them. I am who I am because of all these people.

When I began teaching eighth and tenth grades in Baltimore in the early 1960s, I enjoyed my classroom as my fiefdom, interacting little at all with other teachers, according to prevailing custom. But over recent years my colleagues at Dominican College have taught me the joys of collaboration, and I feel greatly indebted to them: Nancy van Ravenswaay of the North Bay International Studies Project, the late Artelle Farley, Barry Kaufman, Mary Crosby, Madalienne Peters, Kathleen Quigley, Paul Bosque, Sr. Patricia Dougherty, Marlene Jones Schoonover, and Anne Beaufort.

I am also indebted to all those classroom teachers who, over eleven years, have served as master teachers to my student teachers and in whose classrooms I have soaked up the current realities. Linda Danielson will have to represent them all. Linda accepted me in her classroom as co-teacher and collaborated with me in the truest sense of trusting and being honest. This book would never have seen the ink on its pages without her.

My mentor in learning to teach and to write over twenty-two years has been Herb Kohl. No one has influenced me more or given me more sensitive intellectual challenge than he has over our long friendship. His comments on this manuscript helped me make significant improvements. Other helpful readers were Karen Jorgensen, Alice Lucas, Nancy van Ravenswaay, and Susan Hill.

After I drafted my manuscript I discovered two accounts that tell me I am not alone. Thanks to Ginny Seabrook for her work described in "A Teacher Learns in the Context of a Social Studies Workshop," *Making School Reform Work: Lessons From Educators* (Harvard University Press 1992) and to Margot Fortunato Galt for *The Story in History: Writing Your Way into the American Experience* (Teachers and Writers Collaborative 1992).

I am grateful to many people at Heinemann for their expert assistance, especially Toby Gordon for her guidance and encouragement and Nancy Sheridan for steering the manuscript through production.

Most of all I thank my sons, Erik and Ivor, my stepchildren Deborah, Peter, and Daniel, their mates and children, and my incomparable husband, Jack, all of whom share with me in the never-ending teaching and learning.

One

Introduction

When I think about studying history, I remember the opening seminar in my undergraduate honors history class. About fifteen students, including me, sat expectantly around a polished table, watching the balding, twinkley-eyed professor. He surprised us by pulling an Indian-head nickel out of his pants pocket. Setting it on the table before us, he asked us to pretend that we were in the year A.D. 4060 and had found this piece of metal. What could we infer from it about the vanished civilization?

From that class I retained a sense of how fragile is the past, how little of its evidence is left, and how careful we must be when we draw conclusions about history from whatever evidence is available.

In 1961 when I began teaching tenth-grade world history in a Baltimore public school, I relied on the graduate library at Johns Hopkins University for help. To capture my students' attention, I selected from the library anything that might interest them—authentic recruiting posters from World War I, the last letters of German soldiers trapped in Stalingrad in 1944, and poetry of all sorts.

Even as a beginning teacher I knew that students need to have something tangible; they had to see and do something and figure out for themselves the sense of the lesson. I couldn't just stand there and tell them.

I have been teaching history off and on over a forty-year period and have observed other history teachers for about as long. I am certain that ordinary middle and high school students can make great leaps in their understanding of history if teachers can create for their students a workshop environment where they can actually practice being historians.

1

After dreaming about what adolescents might do with history in a workshop setting, I returned to a high school classroom to try my ideas with students. Their work exceeded my dreams. Here is the story created by a tenth-grade girl, Ruth, as part of a six-week unit in world history called "Making Sense of Hitler, the Holocaust, and World War II."

My name is Jan Karski. I worked at the Warsaw ghetto before the Jews' uprising in April of 1943. Because I am Polish, I was not forced to live in the ghetto for the Jews. Instead I lived behind my print shop on the "Aryan side" of Warsaw. In my shop late at night, I would make phony documents for some Jews to escape their gloomy fate. In March and April, many people were being sent to Auschwitz. With my help, the few people that weren't immediately being sent to Auschwitz escaped by the sewers and hid out into the woods. Many of the escapees became the free- dom fighters and fought for any shred of hope to end the Nazis' demented massacre. I knew that what I was doing was forbidden by the Nazis, and I would definitely be executed if caught. But, to me, it was worth sacrificing my life to save the dozens of other lives I helped deliver into "freedom"—away from Hitler's death camps.

Shortly before the Jews' uprising, I helped a small family escape. It was a very rich family before the war, but the Nazis took all their savings, their house, and their business. Everyone was equally poor at the ghetto. There was no classing the people. They all belonged to one class. They were all condemned Jews. I made phony documents for the family, all under the name of Larssen. Their real names would give away their identity—their name of Rothschild.

The night that they were to escape was very cold. It was April 9, 1943. It began to snow as I reached the place that we were to meet. I knew the family was taking a risk by coming to a restaurant on the "Aryan side", but then again, it was a much bigger risk that they were about to take—an escape effort to Sweden.

As I entered the restaurant, The Plaza Bistro, I saw the small family huddled into a small booth, waiting for their food to arrive from the discriminating German waiter. I casually walked over to the manager, seated twenty feet away from the Rothschilds. I handed Mr. Yastrensky the menus I had printed for his res- taurant. As we said our brief goodbyes, I walked toward the bathroom, crossing the path of the Rothschild's table. There, I "accidentally" dropped my hankerchief. As Mr. Rothschild helped me recollect my hankerchief, I quickly handed him the fake documents and passports.

See? It was all really quite easy. No one ever saw what had actually occurred between myself and a stranger. My meetings with the people I helped were never complicated, and I never drew attention to myself or to my secret plans.

Later that night, near the rear end of the restaurant, I personally met with the family. Other than the two parents who I had already met, I was introduced to the two children, Sarah and Joshua. They seemed really close to one another.

Before I had encountered the family in the alley, I heard the mother quietly pleading with the daughter in Yiddish. The son stood solid, even when the father had tried to yell into his face about something I could not understand.

As I walked up to them, they grew silent, and put on fake smiles to pretend that all was well. And now, as we all stood silent, I could tell that the family was holding back on me. Through my endless demands, the son finally broke down, and began to tell me of his plans. Joshua refused to leave the ghetto like his "cowardly" father. Instead, he was to stay in the ghetto and help with the peoples' secret attack. There was word in the bunkers that weapons had been smuggled in to the prisoners. Joshua had already told his friends that he would stay.

I looked over at Mrs. Rothschild's face, stained with free-falling tears. I glanced over at Sarah's face. It was solid with admiration for her brother.

"I'm staying, too!" Sarah blurted out her decision that she had made earlier. I didn't object to their desire to fight for their freedom—it was what I was doing. I smiled and reached out for Mrs. Rothschild's hand; reassurance was the only medicine that would ease her mind now. The Rothschild children would fight for their independence in Warsaw.

The Jews' uprising lasted for three desperate weeks. The Jews' fought as long and as hard as they could. But, in the end, every Jew that had begun the fighting lay dead on the ground. After the revolt, the Warsaw ghetto was burned down to the ground.

A few days before the Warsaw ghetto was burned down, I visited Sarah's room. I looked under the small pillow that once supported her head, and found a small journal that she had recorded her thoughts. When I read it, I cried. The last couple of weeks that I had known her, I grew very fond of her. I felt as if it was my duty to protect her—like she was my own daughter. And when I found out that she had died, I must have felt the pain that Mrs. Rothschild felt when she was told that her daughter wanted to stay and fight like her brother.

I've included some of the excerpts in her diary. They show the strong will of a young woman, fighting alongside her people, joined for one cause—FREEDOM.

April 11, 1943
Tonight, I talked to Joshua about the revolt. I am determined to fight alongside him. For too long, the Jews have absorbed the discrimination. I cannot remember a time when all was well for our family. Soon, we shall have our justice.

April 18, 1943
Joshua tells me our move is tomorrow. I feel excited and nervous. I don't want to die and leave Joshua, or Mamma and Pappa. But, it has been my decision, and the Jewish people are relying on me. I won't let you down!

April 21, 1943
The fighting has been hard. So many people are dead. We've killed some Germans. I feel like I am finally getting my long-awaited revenge on the Germans. Joshua and I have only lost a couple of friends to the cause. We are still going strong!

April 27, 1943
I've reread my last entry. I cannot make sense of the words. How can I go on when Joshua has left me? I am alone. There is no other reason for living. I feel so naive now. What cause could I have been talking of? We are only weak inferior people compared to the Germans.

May 3, 1943
Today, I feel that my will and courage have grown stronger. I killed a young German lieutenant and captured his Luger and ammunition. With his gun and the thirty-five bullets, I feel that I can fight every last German. Moderation, though. Here, in the ghetto, our ammunition is running low. It's funny, though. I remember the look on the young man's face. It was almost innocent and beautiful. But I have no sympathy for the murderers of my people. Because of me, there is one less Jew hater in this world.

May 10, 1943
There are only a few of us left behind, and only one clip of ammunition left. I am determined to fight until death. I shall never regret what I have done for my people and Joshua. If I shall

die, I hope that someone will retrieve this journal and return it to my parents, or to my friend, Jan Karski. If I shall die, I will join Joshua and my people in peace.

That evening, Sarah, along with the last survivors, were smoked out of their bunkers and shot to death. To me, Sarah matured from a naive girl, into an independent woman. I'm sure that the hardest problem she ever faced was to continue to fight even after her brother's death. In my heart, I feel much admiration for the woman I protected so long ago in the Warsaw ghetto. She would have been glad to see the end of the Holocaust, and her ultimate revenge—the end of Hitler's reign.

This story was written in response to my challenge, "Create any fictional character in Hitler's Europe and develop a story about this person. You can choose any role you wish: a Nazi, a non-Nazi German, a Jewish victim, a non-Jewish victim, rescuer, any role you can imagine."

I proposed this challenge based on some assumptions I make about how teenagers think historically. I believe that adolescents, rather than thinking analytically, prefer to identify strongly with heroes and heroines and to explore their own lives and identity, character and convictions, through heroic stories. By their teens, students easily empathize with people who lived in the past, but they focus on their primary task—their own identity formation.

Ruth certainly fulfilled my expectations about how teenagers think about history. She created not one heroic figure, but two—a male and a female. She was able to speak in the voice of each character, while exploring her own role and gender, defining herself as one who would fight with weapons for her convictions. Ruth used accurate historical information as background for her exploration of character. I couldn't hope for more.

Ruth's story demonstrates that she practiced many historical skills during this unit of work. She acquired information about the Warsaw Ghetto, Jewish resistance, Auschwitz, and Yiddish. She empathized with Jewish parents and a Polish rescuer. She examined moral dilemmas in history by constructing fictional characters who acted in accurate settings. She chose her own story and projected herself onto her characters, examining her own growing identity, imagining what choices she would have made during the Nazi period, and how she might act if ever faced with similar dilemmas. She went through the whole process of writing: reading, researching, drafting, revising, receiving feedback, and presenting the final story both in writing and orally.

How did I help Ruth? I established her classroom as a workshop in which students could imitate graduate school methodology or professional historians. I asked Ruth and her classmates to leave their textbooks at home, and I brought in a variety of primary sources for them to use. I challenged them to write stories rather than reports, and I went slower than usual, providing more time for reading, writing, and reflecting than is usually allowed in the history curriculum. I brought to history class everything I knew about the process of writing and, over several weeks, gave Ruth and her classmates a chance to give and receive feedback on their stories and to revise them.

This complex process of instruction I call history workshop. This book describes what history workshop might be and how to carry it out in the real world of bells and students. When I began this work, I was teaching education in college, not history in high school. I was observing student teachers in middle and high school, but I was not in a high school classroom every day.

Aware that my hypothesis needed testing, in the spring of 1991, I offered an experimental college course, History 173: Postwar U.S., which focused on three topics: the Cold War, the Civil Rights Movement, and the Vietnam War. As a final project each student interviewed someone who had been involved in the Vietnam War and presented these oral histories in class. Students chose people from a wide range of roles: naval officer, female nurse-volunteer, drafted combat soldier addicted to drugs, U.S. Aid official, Air Force technician. When each had presented their findings, the class had been exposed to a breathtaking collage of experience and interpretation.

This success bolstered my confidence in the idea of history workshop, but I knew that I had to return to a high school classroom to confirm whether or not the approach could be implemented there. The logistics were not immediately apparent. My college needed me to direct its secondary teaching program, and I didn't want to take leave from that job to teach high school full time. The problem could be solved if I found a high school teacher who agreed to co-teach one class with me and to follow my lead in planning the lessons.

What teacher would agree to this? Who would be compatible with me? Who would be willing to take the risks I knew were inherent in what I planned to do?

Raising these questions brought an answer. I decided to approach a skilled tenth-grade teacher, Linda Danielson, whom I had met the year before. Linda was intrigued with the idea of co-teaching. She read some of my draft chapters about the idea of history workshop and said, "Sure. Let's try it."

Linda teaches at Novato High School in Novato, California. This is a suburban area of Marin County, on the peninsula about twenty-five miles north of San Francisco.

Novato High School, which had 1100 students during the 1991-1992 school year, has a large Caucasian group with diverse minorities: 82 percent white, 6 percent Asian, 7 percent Hispanic, 4 percent Black, and 1 percent other. A well-organized Black Parents Association carefully monitors alleged racist incidents that occur at the school and presses the principal to hold in-service training for teachers in intercultural sensitivity. Sixty-four percent of Novato High's graduates go on to higher education of some kind.

In the spring of 1991, Linda and I agreed to co-teach our experimental unit the following spring semester, in 1992. We met regularly from October through December to plan the unit, which we called "Making Sense of Hitler, the Holocaust, and World War II." We implemented our plans from January 14 to February 28, 1992.

I write about our experiment as a journey to discover what history workshop might look like in high school. First we had the idea, then put it into practice step by step. We reflected on the idea again. Only then could I identify what seem to be the major instructional components of implementing history workshop in middle and high school. To provide markers for the trail ahead, here are some of the elements:

1. Conception of history
   History is seen as competing stories told by people who interpret facts about the past as they are known, instead of being seen as a fixed, correct account.

2. Primary sources
   Students explore the materials themselves, rather than being told what to believe.

3. Multiple perspectives
   Many interpretations of the past are presented—not just one viewpoint—and students are encouraged to think about history in different ways.

4. Journal writing
   Students are asked to write about questions or dilemmas related to the historical materials they study, rather than responding to random quotes.

5. History talk groups
   Students form small discussion groups after they read primary
   sources to practice identifying what seem to be the facts and
   asserting their ideas and interpretations of them.

6. Lectures and class discussions
   Information is presented in lecture format and whole-class discussions, but only after students generate their own questions
   about the material.

7. Process writing assignment
   A unit-long writing assignment is given and procedures for effective process writing are followed. Students may choose from a
   variety of genres.

This book presents a set of ideas about teaching history and one
instance of their implementation. Chapter 2 describes the idea of
history workshop, and chapters 3 and 4 detail how Linda and I put
the idea into practice. Chapter 5 contains stories written by several
students and their insights into the process of writing historical fiction. Chapter 6 analyzes what seem to be the major instructional
components of history workshop. The final chapter, *What's Next?*,
suggests some ways history workshop can be explored further. I hope
this book will be the first of many that describe what teenagers can do
with history as teachers develop the trust and confidence to set up
their classrooms as workplaces for young historians.

Two

The Idea of History Workshop

When a typical history classroom meets, the teacher usually asks everyone to take out pencils and notebooks and prepare to take notes on whatever the day's topic; for instance, the French Revolution. Most students comply. Often, several students in the back never manage to open their notebooks or, if they do, slip in something else to read.

Normally the teacher talks for twenty-five minutes, answers a few questions from students, and poses a few for student volunteers. Students take notes with varying degrees of enthusiasm, which declines noticeably from front seats to back ones.

For the rest of the period the teacher often hands out a worksheet with terms and dates to identify. Students begin work, find the answers in the textbook, and write them on the sheet. Whatever they don't finish in class will be homework that evening.

The textbook, which students are supposed to carry back and forth from home to locker to class, weighs five or six pounds. Usually it contains thirty to thirty-five chapters, just enough to set a pace of about one per week.

In many classes, students are given a test every Friday, which includes a selection of terms and dates from their weeks' worksheets to be identified from memory. By the end of the semester many of the students hate history—if they didn't already.

To be fair, this is a worst-case scenario. In the schools I visit I sometimes see lively discussions, role playing, or imaginative writing assignments ("Pretend you are the girl in the foreground of the photo of factory workers. Write down what you imagine she would put in her diary at night"). But often these are special assignments used to break the monotony of the regular fare.

9

Other contemporary views confirm my observations. John Goodlad's data gleaned from more than one-thousand classrooms validate the popular image of a teacher standing or sitting in front of a class imparting knowledge to a group of students. Goodlad found that explaining and lecturing constitute the most frequent teaching activities, increasing in use from the lower elementary grades through high school. In middle schools teachers spend substantial time observing students work or monitoring their seatwork. Except in art, vocational education, and physical education, students are seldom actively involved in learning. The emotional tone is neither joyful nor punitive, but rather flat. Students rank social studies/history low when they list the order of favorite school subjects (1984). Although this data is eight years old as I write, it has not changed that much.

I am struck foremost by the boredom, disengagement, and passivity of students in a typical history classroom. Teachers do most of the activity; students are recorders and receptacles. If students do nothing but record lectures and copy definitions from textbooks, how can they possibly become interested in history or begin to understand what it is?

Perhaps teachers feel compelled to lecture because of the staggering volume of facts that history includes. John and Evelyn Dewey observed eighty years ago in *Schools of Tomorrow:*

> The one [change] possibly most significant from the point of view of education is the incredible increase in the number of facts that must be part of the mental furniture of anyone who meets even the ordinary situation of life successfully. There are so many that any attempt to teach them all from text-books in school hours would be simply ridiculous. But the schools, instead of facing this frankly and then changing their curriculum so that they could teach pupils how to learn from the world itself, have gone on bravely teaching as many facts as possible. (1915, p. 307)

Over the years there has been confusion about the primary purpose of teaching history. Before the overwhelming social, national, and global changes that occurred during the last forty years, there seems to have been agreement that the primary purpose of a history curriculum should be the inculcation of nationalism and the preparation of citizens. Secondary purposes included understanding facts and concepts, clarifying values, and exploring personal identity.

Now, however, the teaching of nationalism has given way to the exploration of ethnic and gender identities and/or to developing global solidarity. Students, faced with still more facts, are given fewer ways of understanding them.

Since the older, accepted understanding of the facts has broken apart, however, new syntheses are being developed. Now there is a chance for history teachers to invite their students to help make sense of the facts, to put them together in fresh ways, and in doing so to practice history themselves.

But students cannot practice history until they unlearn what they already think about it. Plainly put by University of Chicago historian Tom Holt, high school students often conceive of history

> ... as the ordering of already known facts into agreed-upon chronologies. They think of history as sealed off both from the lives of ordinary people and from questions about how the particulars of everyday life become the generalizations of historical knowledge. For many students, only a fiction writer shapes and interprets—not a historian. And above all, they think they are the consumers, not the makers, of history. It is there: fixed, final, and waiting to be read. (p.2)

Teaching and learning history in secondary school won't change until teachers and students conceive of history in a way very different from that just described. Many teachers' idea of history is rooted in the nineteenth and early twentieth centuries, when historians strove to be objective and believed that they could actually describe the past as it really was; that history could be fixed and final.

Current historians, however, are ready to admit that, while the past may exist objectively as what really happened, history—how human beings remember and describe the past—can never wholly capture that objectivity. History is stories told by people about what happened, and different groups of people tell different narratives depending on their perspectives and experiences. Struggles ensue about which narratives will be accepted by a society as the "correct" ones. The way people put the facts together and the struggle over which are correct reflect the political, economic, and social issues and ideologies of the time. This current understanding of history acknowledges the role of interpretation in the construction of history and accepts that every person can and must be his or her own historian.

With this analysis of traditional history teaching, I began to explore metaphors that might lead me to a new approach. Occasional effective lessons no longer satisfied me. As long as the format remained the creation of single, scintillating lessons, the burden still rested on the teacher. I sought a process that would shift the burden and the learning to the students.

When I reviewed my own experience as a history student, I realized that, with the single exception of a seventh-grade project on local history, I was bored with history until I majored in it in college. Only when I reached upper-division courses did the excitement and meaning of history open up for me. "Why not let younger students do what we did at college and graduate levels?" I asked.

Science teachers go to great lengths to set up labs for their students, so that they can work in the same way that professional scientists work. Music teachers organize bands and orchestras to imitate adult ones. Art teachers create studios. Math teachers—well, they do their best to get their students to practice the procedures of mathematicians.

In the past ten years the most significant instructional changes in elementary and secondary instruction have occurred in the language arts, and this has been accomplished by teachers who establish a writing process for their students that imitates what professional adult writers do. This overall philosophy, known as whole language, includes both writing process and writing workshop.

So, what is the relationship of history to whole language and the language arts? In the high school curriculum they are almost always considered separate subjects; only in middle school are they sometimes scheduled together as a core period.

But are they separate subjects? Can history be carried on without language? Of course not. Separating these subjects is nonsense. History *is* language arts and can only be created through language. The past may exist, in itself, as events and artifacts, but history is created by people using language.

From here I made the leap. Why not teach history as a workshop analogous to writing workshop? Why not bring to young people the process through which professional historians learn and work, just as writing workshop reproduces the process through which professional writers write?

Historians are writers who accept a basic constraint on their work—it has to conform to what is known about the past through rigorous, scientific study. Beyond that, historians are not limited; they write in many genres, and they go through the same process as any other writer: experience, prewriting, choosing a topic, drafting, soliciting response, revising, editing, proofing, illustrating, publishing, celebrating.

Before I jumped in to create a process in history class analogous to the process that writers and historians share in creating a finished product, I wanted to think more about this analogy and to read what others have said about how children and young adults learn history.

Young People As Historians

Most children don't enjoy learning historical names and dates. Names and dates are analogous to what used to be called subskills in reading, like decoding or sounding out words or syllables. Focusing on these subskills does not result in reading comprehension. Children can learn to sound out the words without any idea of their meaning. For reading skills to be practiced and absorbed, the focus needs to be on making sense of the material. Then, all the skills are learned as part of a larger, meaningful activity. Similarly, young people can learn historical facts to pass a test without any real idea of what they mean.

I began to realize that students might learn history better if they were given a chance to make sense of the past, to create their own meaning, to write and construct their own beliefs about history rather than to focus on the acquisition of facts.

But how do children learn to make sense of the past? How do they develop as historians as they mature from early childhood to early adulthood? Certainly teenagers are not ready to be professional historians; what are their characteristic ways of thinking historically?

In answering these questions I started from the belief that every person is a historian. It seems clear that we humans construct our sense of self from our personal, day-to-day history. If we develop amnesia and cannot remember our personal history, we can no longer function as full human beings.

Very young children must develop their basic sense of self, learning that they are different from Mommy and Daddy, that they persist from day to day, that they have wills and intentions of their own. Children become acquainted with the members of their extended family, fit into a community of friends, and begin their store of conscious memories.

Once children reach school age, how do they develop historical thinking? Surely, I thought, something in the research literature would tell me about how children learn history. Are there stages they go through? How is their thinking about history related to adult thinking? What is the continuum from five year old to twenty-five year old?

I found, to my surprise, that no one yet knows much about how children learn history. Pioneering studies conducted in England focused on how students understand chronology (Oakden and Sturt, 1922; Bradley, 1947). Studies made between 1955 and 1980, influenced by the ideas of Jean Piaget, suggested that chronological and logical capacity develop late in children; there seems to be a leap around age eleven, but full ability to think historically does not click in until age sixteen or seventeen. (The work of Roy N. Hallam, 1967, 1972, is the best known of this research. The literature on children's conception of time, as well as on learning and teaching history in general, has been thoroughly reviewed by Matthew T. Downey and Linda S. Levstik, 1991.)

More recently, some investigators, especially Kieran Egan, are looking at one historical ability that young children have in abundance—imagination. Children have no trouble listening to stories and re-enacting historical situations. Perhaps they are not such slow learners in history as we have thought, but are affected by teachers who focus too much on the logic and chronology of history (1979, 1986, 1990).

Researchers who focused on the logic and chronology of history often were men, say the women investigators who have shown that girls' thinking is different from that of boys. Carol Gilligan, Nona P. Lyons and Trudy J. Hanmer suggest that adolescent women's ways of knowing contrast with those of adolescent men. Women are interdependent and connected with others, instead of being autonomous and separate in relation to others as men tend to be. Women want to understand situations, contexts, and people and seek to convince by motives and the particulars of lives. Men tend to find answers to questions and to convince by argument and logic (1989).

But researchers have not yet studied enough about how teenagers think about history to form any firm conclusions. We need longitudinal studies, which would follow children from early elementary grades through high school and college and would look at multiple aspects of historical thinking. Until these studies are made we cannot yet describe general patterns in the historical thinking of middle and high school students.

Meanwhile, to teach I must draw some conclusions about what adolescents are doing when they think about history. The teen years are a time of conscious identity formation. In all cultures, but especially in U.S. culture, teenagers must individuate themselves from their families and be ready to strike out on their own by their early twenties. They must try to analyze what groups their families belong to and where in the bewildering array of possible choices they fit and belong. They must establish their identity in part by understanding how their families fit into public history and by choosing what of their history to reject and what to retain.

To achieve this understanding of how their families fit into history, adolescents must make great leaps to extend their memory of other peoples and places. Schools tend to present to students, in

textbooks, versions of the facts already neatly assembled and interpreted. Often young people have trouble fitting their own family
history into the public text, and even if they are able to do so in some
way, they are not expected to make any interpretation of the public
facts for themselves. The text provides the interpretation that students are expected to acquire, presumably for the purpose of molding
them into loyal citizens of their country. But unless students receive
help from their families in figuring out where they fit into history,
they often seem "lost" at sea. Schools seldom present history to
students as a tool for making sense of their lives, even though this
seems to be education's primary task.

From my own experience I know that teenagers can feel a strong
empathy with historical characters. They like to hear about individual stories of courage, challenge, pain, and triumph. By learning
about people in the past, they identify and work through personal
decisions and issues. Adolescents like to know facts, information,
and even chronology—not as abstract material, but as connected to
real people in the past and to their own questions and decisions.
They have no trouble imagining history when it is presented in this
way. They like to interpret it and make sense of it when their teachers
do not dish it out prepackaged to be swallowed whole.

My own understanding of teenage learning is confirmed by two
current theorists, Kieran Egan, professor of education at Simon Fra-
zier University in Vancouver, Canada, and Howard Gardner, professor of education at Harvard University. Egan unabashedly rejects the
logic and cognitive emphasis of Piaget for a position that emphasizes
the imaginative and the affective faculties as the most active ones for
young people. In *Teaching as Storytelling* (1986) Egan proposes organizing the whole primary curriculum in a narrative mode, around
polarities such as good and evil, or survival and destruction. In
*Romantic Understanding: The Development of Rationality and
Imagination, Ages 8-15* (1990) he suggests that there are four distinct
stages of understanding that characterize human development:

1. the mythic stage (up to about six or seven),
2. the romantic stage (from seven or eight to about sixteen),
3. the philosophic stage (sixteen through twenty), and
4. the ironic stage (maturity).

In the mythic stage children are interested in stories that involve
a dramatic struggle between opposites, such as good and evil or
danger and security. They don't care whether these struggles are
real or imagined. In the romantic stage realism becomes important because children and adolescents want to hear about courageous

individuals who struggle with real problems, testing the limits of what is possible in the real world. In the romantic stage young people search for identity by associations with the transcendent qualities of historical figures. Not until the philosophic stage do young people search for general patterns and overall explanations in history, and by the ironic stage they settle for the particularity of historical events.

Howard Gardner, studying the development of children's thought (1992), recognizes that by age six children have developed powerful theories to explain how the world, both past and present, works. Teachers tend not to recognize these theories, believing that they can just pour the facts in without activating the thinking already going on. Because the new information often is not connected to what students already think, they frequently don't adjust their theories and don't really understand. When they leave the classroom, the students easily revert to their six-year-old explanations. Gardner documents this assertion more fully in subjects other than history, but concludes with the same plea as I do: as teachers, let's find ways to connect our materials to what children already think and focus on meaning and understanding as our primary goals.

Constructing Historical Meaning

What would it mean to ask students to take a more active role in constructing their own interpretations of history? Again, I thought about how secondary teachers teach literature. The ones I observe do not usually stand up and talk about John Steinbeck and the meaning of *Of Mice and Men*, not for too long, anyway. English teachers ask students to open the book and start reading. They expect students to discuss what the text means; most of them negotiate with their students the meaning of an author's story, rather than simply imposing their own interpretation.

But this contrasts starkly with history class, where many teachers tell their students what history means. Frequently heated discussions of current social and political issues occur, but seldom are there arguments over how the past should be interpreted.

Yet students think about history differently than adults, and many of them want to think for themselves. They know there is more than one way to interpret past events. They find it boring to be stuffed with facts and conclusions, just as they would be bored in literature class if they couldn't read *Of Mice and Men* for themselves.

What could be done in history class, I asked, to help students construct their own meaning? Textbooks seem to stand in the way; they either make an interpretation that remains hidden or they make no interpretation except in the selection of facts they string together. I felt certain that the first step must be to let students go to primary sources. Only by responding to original material could students begin to expand their imagination about the past and develop their own beliefs about history.

Using original sources and local sources are not new ideas in history teaching. They have played an honorable part of the progressive position in educational theory and practice. Karen Jorgensen-Esmaili traces this story in her article, "Another Look at Community History" (1988), in which she finds four periods when educators showed particular interest in primary sources and local history: 1885–1897, the Great Depression, 1945–1965, including the inquiry method, and in the late 1970s.

In my early teaching I invented ways to use different kinds of primary sources. Once I played Tchaikovsky's 1812 Overture for five classes in one day, complete with an analysis of the musical themes. I never wanted to hear it again. Other times I brought in artifacts; I photocopied excerpts from autobiographies. But most often, I presented poetry—it was short, powerful, and easy to reproduce for class copies.

But in my early teaching I went at this hit or miss, instinctively staying away from ponderous, dull documents, but lacking a comprehensive sense of how many kinds of primary sources there are to choose from. In planning history workshop I defined primary sources as any material created at the time of an event, or later from memory by someone involved in the event. When I listed all the varieties of primary sources available in our culture, these were my categories:

- artifacts: any objects made by people
- visual images: photos, drawings, maps
- written primary sources: diaries, biographies, firsthand accounts, oral histories, poetry, speeches
- recordings: oral histories, music
- living people

This list showed me that, with such a richness of resources, I didn't need to start with the text at all but could use it as a supplement, a reference. My students could go straight to the sources; they could choose what aspects of history on which to focus; they could tell me what it all meant—if only I could be patient and silent enough.

Comparing a history workshop with a writing workshop, I saw that these primary sources could provide for students the experience that constitutes the first step in process writing. After this initial experience with the sources, the students could take the next steps in constructing their own meaning—talking with each other and with me and then writing and discussing their writing.

Writing, I had observed, didn't happen often in history class. When it did, it usually took the form of answering questions or writing a report, possibly a research paper or a book report for extra credit.

But I also knew, from personal experience, that reports and research papers may be more part of the problem than of the solution. In them the writer is taught to objectify history, to depersonalize it, to remove himself or herself from it in order to present it as much as possible without bias. While this may be the duty of a professional historian, it does not encourage personal understanding. It masks the personal involvement. It emphasizes logical thinking. It seems unlikely to be the most powerful and appropriate form for many high school writers of history, most of whom are still in their romantic stage, by Egan's analysis.

But even among adults, most people prefer to read history as a story rather than as a research report. If historians want to reach an audience beyond that of professional historians, they write in various narrative genres: oral history, historical fiction, biography, murder mysteries set in past settings. Why shouldn't teenagers have the same range of genres from which to choose and practice?

As I analyzed these forms of writing, I made a distinction between narrative (a story with characters and plot) and exposition (a report or an essay that explains). I realized that most reading (textbooks) and most writing (reports) in history class are expository in nature. But I also knew from experience that narrative is more interesting and accessible to students than is exposition. Thirty years ago I taught history as a Saturday serial to my tenth-grade classes, using a "cliff hanger" at the end of each period so they would come back eager to hear what happened next. Students who had been absent would rush back, asking, "Mrs. Brown, who won the war?" Somehow, they could not figure out the answer from the textbook; they wanted to hear it from me. For implementing history workshop I resolved to put lots more story into history, both in what I asked students to read and to write.

I wanted to open up the writing so that students could choose both their topics and their genres. I wanted them to present their writing to response groups and to persist with their pieces, revising, researching, making more sense of the past's unlimited complexity.

Putting history workshop into practice would involve me, I realized, in a major shift in attitude both toward history and toward students. I would have to give over a good bit of my control of the subject matter. I would have to listen respectfully to students and pick up their questions, interests, and opinions. I would have to negotiate with them about the meaning of events. When they gave an unexpected response, I couldn't just say, "You're mistaken." I would have to consider their answers and respond with questions to keep them thinking. In short, I would have to give more ownership of the material to the students than teachers customarily do. I believed I could do this, but how would students respond? Parents? The principal?

After thinking through the idea of history workshop, four features seemed essential to me:

1. using primary sources,
2. asking students to write as much as they read,
3. emphasizing stories and narration at least as much as exposition, and
4. listening to students to give them more ownership of the material.

My thinking included vivid images of the possible difficulties in carrying out history workshop in public schools. Primary sources might be hard to collect and care for; students might resist after years of studying history otherwise; surely it might take more time than the curriculum allowed. The structure of middle and high school seems highly inimical to the implementation of history workshop. As soon as I had enticed thirty students into working attentively, I imagined, the bell would ring, and thirty more would rush in.

But I also had images of the possible payoffs—students excited, making sense of their own lives in historical perspective; teachers excited, watching history come to life in their students. Once the idea of history workshop hit me, I wanted to see what would happen if I carried it out with as little compromise as possible.

Chapter Three

Planning for History Workshop in High School

The thought of implementing history workshop in high school definitely made me anxious. My own teaching experience and that of my student teachers reminded me of the daily routines of high school. Bells every fifty minutes. Thirty new students rushing in as each class departs. Frequent interruptions by the P.A. Colleagues in the department who stay together on the material so that they can get through the textbook at the same pace, week by week. Students absorbed in their own worlds. This scene didn't seem a likely place for imaginative, reflective discussion and writing.

Beginning to make concrete plans helped me relax. Linda Danielson and I started our planning with the *History-Social Science Framework for California Public Schools (1988)*, which outlines the structure of history and social science classes for all grades in California. Linda has always followed it quite faithfully, as her principal expects. For tenth-grade world history, the *Framework* specifies:

World History, Culture, and Geography:
The Modern World

1. Unresolved Problems of the Modern World
2. Connecting with Past Learnings: The Rise of Democratic Ideas
3. The Industrial Revolution
4. The Rise of Imperialism and Colonialism: A Case Study of India
5. World War I and Its Consequences
6. Totalitarianism in the Modern World: Nazi Germany and Stalinist Russia

7. World War II: Its Causes and Consequences
8. Nationalism in the Contemporary World (case studies of the Soviet Union and China, Israel and Syria, Ghana and South Africa, and Mexico and Brazil)

For the history workshop, I wanted to pick one topic in the year's scheduled work and create more time for it by condensing the time for topics covered before and after. As we looked at the topics that usually fall in the spring semester, *Nazi Germany* jumped out at us. It held high interest for us; we knew it would have high interest for our students; and we knew it would be easy to find primary sources, photos, and other materials about it. Decision made.

As we worked with the calendar and the topics, we realized that we needed to cover the Holocaust, too, and that doing so would include World War II. So we switched our title from *The Rise of Nazism* to *Hitler, the Holocaust, and World War II*.

It is noteworthy that *History-Social Science Framework* specifies that the German Holocaust should be viewed in relation to the previous one perpetrated on Armenians and as a model for other despots, such as Pol Pot in Cambodia. It does not mention the Atlantic crossing of Africans as a genocide or the destruction of Native Americans. But the *Framework* does make clear genocide is what matters and that the German Holocaust is one instance of it (1988, p.87).

In order to create five or six weeks for our unit, Linda agreed to modify her year's schedule by finishing the *World War I and Its Consequences* unit in the first semester rather than the beginning of the second semester. By consolidating *The Industrial Revolution* and *The Rise of Imperialism and Colonialism* into four weeks instead of the usual six or seven weeks, she felt students would get what they needed, and they would be ready to begin *Nazi Germany* at the beginning of the second semester. Linda included *Stalinist Russia* as a consequence of World War I, so that we would not need to include it in our unit.

The other decision we made in May concerned the writing assignment. For me history workshop meant giving the students leeway to write in many more genres than those to which they were usually limited. Specifically, I didn't want to assign them a report or research paper. Did this mean they couldn't write a report if they wanted to? Should we leave the assignment wide open and let them choose which genre they preferred? I liked this plan but felt, since I didn't know the students, I couldn't judge their readiness for it. If wide-open choice were to succeed, they would need prior experience with at least several different genres, and Linda doubted whether this was the case.

We decided that it would be most effective to focus on one genre that we would teach students, and that this genre would be fictional biography. Students could choose any character in Hitler's Europe and work out a story of that person some time between 1930 and 1945. They could read biographies and autobiographies, fictional and nonfictional, to help them get ideas.

By agreeing to this assignment to create a fictional biography, Linda and I found ourselves in harmony about our fundamental conception of history. If we still thought that history referred to the study of what kings, queens, presidents, and armies did in the past, we could not have agreed that this was an appropriate assignment. But we have both been influenced by the revolution in historical thinking that has occurred since World War II, and we both believe that history includes people's everyday lives. This assignment reveals one of the many ways that our conception of history affects our teaching.

In October Linda and I met again. By then she had her classes for the year—one in English and four tenth-grade world history classes. Linda chose for us a class that met from 9:10 A.M. to 10:00 A.M. and had a wide mix of students who worked well together. The class included eleven boys, fourteen girls, no African Americans, one girl whose parents were from India, two Asian American girls, with the rest European American.

At our October meeting we brainstormed what firsthand materials we might use: Adolph Hitler, *Mein Kampf*; Studs Terkel, *The Good War*; Elie Wiesel, *Night*; Ruth Minsky Sender, *The Cage*; and Anne Frank, *The Diary of Anne Frank*. Linda thought that probably two-thirds of the students would already have read the diary. But that raised another question—could we persuade the English department to work with us and assign some Holocaust literature during the same weeks we were presenting our unit?

The idea seemed simple enough, but we knew it wasn't. Linda was aware that the English department followed a fixed list of books for each grade, from which they would be loathe to deviate. We decided we had enough work without involving another department; that could come later when we felt we knew what we were doing.

At this same meeting we made our initial stab at blocking out our lessons. We agreed on this general sequence: first, we would ask the students about what they wanted to know; second, we would present primary documents and basic facts and make the writing assignment; third, students would read fictional biographies and work in writing groups; fourth, while this continued we would introduce more documents and facts; and, fifth, students would present their work. Since we were still assuming a five-week unit, here are my notes of how we laid it out:

- Week 1: formulate questions; read primary documents; go over basic facts and maps
- Week 2: continue; make writing assignment; brainstorm possible characters
- Week 3: read fictional biography; work in writers' groups; individual conferences
- Week 4: present more facts and documents; interview survivor (?)
- Week 5: require presentations by writing groups

We ended this meeting by giving ourselves an assignment: decide what the basic facts are and what primary documents we want to use.

I spent the dark, chilly November evenings reading before the fireplace. My limited background in Hitler and the Holocaust included twice teaching a high school course thirty years ago. I had read Anne Frank's diary and several accounts by survivors. Once I attended a workshop for teachers about teaching the Holocaust, conducted by a group called "Facing History and Ourselves." I started my reading with the handbook they provided: Margot Stern Strom and William S. Parsons, *Facing History and Ourselves: Holocaust and Human Behavior.*

This turned out to be a treasure chest of primary documents appropriate for high school and ready to be used. I had only to choose from the rich array: there were plenty for a semester—or even a year—of study. It was clear that finding materials for this unit would not be a problem.

I had one negative response to *Facing History and Ourselves*— the fate of homosexuals under Nazism wasn't mentioned anywhere. One paragraph that listed groups caught in the Nazi plan of extermination included the single word, "homosexuals." Otherwise, not a clue to the persecution of homosexuals.

Since this seemed to me a contradiction of the basic message that we must face the truth about the past and ourselves, I called the office of Intentional Educations. They explained that they now considered this omission a serious oversight. Since this book came out in 1982, much more has been learned about the fate of homosexuals under Hitler and they are preparing a new edition of their book for next year to include more about non-Jewish victims. They promised to send me the draft materials about homosexuals, which they would be happy for me to pilot.

I found *Night* by Wiesel and *The Cage* by Sender to be magnificent human documents, bound to enthrall students. As I studied I also discussed with my friends the endless questions: Should we see the Holocaust primarily as an anti-Jewish event or as a racial purification event? Does any animal species other than humans ever turn against itself like this? Could it happen here?

By November Linda and I were ready to outline a sequence of specific lessons. We both are planners; we need to foresee what each day will bring. We can always change the plan as students respond, but since we have to end by a certain date, we want to work out a sequence of topics and decide the pacing.

One important question we faced was whether or not to require all students to read one book, probably *Night* or *The Cage*. Doing this would provide a common core of knowledge and vicarious experience, but we didn't have enough copies or enough time.

We decided to require only short documents that we could photocopy and read in class or assign as homework. Book-length documents would be optional extra credit. We planned to round up several copies of the most appealing stories, which students could borrow, and we would find time for the students who did read an optional book to share it with their classmates. This way all the students could become familiar with several books. We knew we would never run out of things to do in class.

Linda and I discussed what it meant to be co-teachers. Neither of us had done this before. Linda was certainly the class teacher, but we wanted the students to view me as more than a continual guest. How could we help the students accept me as their teacher, too? We decided that both of us should teach, alternating pieces of each lesson. This method would actively involve us in each day's presentation. We also decided that both of us would give the grades, since that is the bottom line for students. We would read all their written work and find some way to agree on the grade.

Linda announced a revision in our planned schedule. Since she was ahead on her first semester's schedule, we could start the week before final exams then pick up again the week after. This would give us six whole weeks and a chance for students to mull over introductory ideas while they worked on finals.

Linda brought her usual planning format, an 8 1/2" x 11" page for each month, and we laid out the lessons in pencil so that we could easily adjust them. We found that we were alternating six components: (1) journal writing, (2) content lectures, (3) photos and videos, (4) primary documents and talk groups, (5) writing groups, and (6) student presentations.

As Linda and I decided the sequence of these lessons, we made clear to each other what we considered important. I felt strongly that we must begin by soliciting from the students what they already knew about the topic and, most important, what they wanted to know. Linda urged that class begin each day with journal writing;

they were used to this procedure, and she needed ten minutes of quiet to get her work done. We both believed that our students should learn the basic facts, dates, terms, and vocabulary about our topic expected in any history course. We selected from all facts a minimal core that students would be required to know and remember. These facts would serve as the framework on which to hang more and more information. Since students wouldn't have the textbook to provide this information, we felt responsible to supply it in minilessons, or minilectures.

Actually, our plan already contained one important revision from earlier discussions. Eager to show the video, *The Wave*, based on a short story by Ron Jones, we had initially scheduled it for the first week to engage students in questions about how and why people supported Hitler. *The Wave* is about a teacher who organized his class into a powerful group that operated on mottoes like "Strength Through Discipline," and "Strength Through Community," to show his students the appeal of Nazism. His students got very involved in the Wave. Only one or two students dissented; the rest felt secure and empowered by belonging to the group. The teacher brought the experiment to a close by showing a documentary of the Nuremberg rallies, which the students recognize as mirroring what they have done.

I felt strongly that we needed more time in the first week to learn about Hitler himself, so we decided to show *The Wave* during the last week, when we would discuss under what conditions it could happen again.

Now we had a sequence of lessons, but still we had made no decisions about what specific documents to use. I gave Linda copies of my first selection of documents from *Facing History and Ourselves*, but there were still far too many. For our next meeting, we assigned ourselves the selection of specific documents for specific lessons and the creation of a bibliography for ourselves and our students.

Sometime in early December I dropped by Novato High School to chat with the librarian, Karen Peterson—I knew she had a special interest in the Holocaust. Karen knew this subject cold. She brought to my attention the *Maus* books by Art Spiegelman and urged me to read them. She volunteered to raid other school libraries in Marin County; to set up a cart full of books that our students could check out; to whip up a two-page, annotated bibliography of the best and most appropriate books as a guide for our students; and to come to our class to preview her own favorite selections. This assistance proved invaluable; the task of locating supporting materials was basically lifted from us.

During our December 30 meeting we agreed on which documents to use. Since I wanted students to be able to talk about what they read, we decided to form History Talk Groups to allow students to discuss a document immediately after the reading. Students would choose a facilitator and a recorder for each group and report their interpretations back to the whole class.

We also discussed how to create a setting in which students could present their own writing. We had decided that, in addition to History Talk Groups, there would be Writers' Groups of four students, different from the talk groups. At the end of the unit each student would be provided time to share his or her story with the whole class.

Finally, we discussed the well-known fact that effective teachers model what they teach. If we really wanted to generate great student writing, we had better do some ourselves. Our eyeballs rolled, but we overcame our reluctance to expose ourselves in this way, and started to share with each other what we might like to write about. Soon we cut this off, realizing that we should save the sharing as a spontaneous class activity where it would model for students how to think about roles they might like to explore.

The final version of history workshop looked like this:

Making Sense of Hitler and the Holocaust

Week 1:	**1.** Intro to Project; Generating Questions	Jan. 14
	2. Idea of Race	
	3. *Mein Kampf*	
	4. Hitler as a Person: Video	
	5. Intro to Writing	
Week 2:	**6.** Kristallnacht	Jan. 27
	7. How did Jews resist? Warsaw Ghetto	
	8. Concentration camps	
	9. Resistance: who helped?	
	10. Possible roles; character due	
Week 3:	**11.** Lecture: Beginning of WW II	Feb. 3
	12. Lecture: Sequence of WW II	
	13. Concentration Camps: Homosexuals	
	14. Writing Groups	
	15. Fact and map text	

Week 4:   Holiday   Feb. 10
           16. Individual Writing Conferences
           17. Last Day in Camps
           18. Guest survivor
           19. End of War and Nuremberg Trials/Fact test
Week 5:   **20.** *The Wave* video   Feb. 17
           21. Neo Nazism: Can It Happen Again?
           22. Read Around
           23. Individual Stories
           24. Individual Stories
Week 6:   Holiday   Feb 24
           25. Stories
           26. Stories
           27. Stories
           28. Closure and Evaluation

In summary, we gave ourselves a nine-month lead for planning. We mentioned our topic to friends and librarians, who fed us ideas and sources. We trusted our serendipity to bring to our attention all kinds of resources we had not noticed at first. We spent eight hours in four meetings on planning. All this proved not only feasible within our busy schedules but refreshing and invigorating; we began to count our planning time as doing something for ourselves.

After our planning was completed, I thought, "How are we going to know if we are succeeding? What are our objectives here? Why didn't I write my objectives first, then my plans?"

Why? Because first I needed to work through what I wanted to do in the classroom. From my plans I quickly inferred my objectives; once stated, I then used the objectives to revise and tighten up my classroom plans.

These were the goals for our students:

Students will be able to

- learn the basic facts about Hitler, the Holocaust, and World War II.
- work from primary documents and identify each document's perspective.
- explore and defend their own feelings and opinions in an extended piece of nonexpository writing.
- create their own interpretations of history.

My goals included to:

- achieve the student goals above, as measured by student work.
- describe how students react when given more ownership of their history studies and describe the level of tenth-grade student work.
- demonstrate that the history workshop approach allows students to be more involved in their history studies than usual, as measured by observed student behavior and by student testimony.

This is not a controlled study. How students develop their skills and understanding of history can only be documented longitudinally, following individual students from the early school years to adulthood. Such studies are beginning to be made. This piece of work will simply provide an introductory description of what typical tenth-grade history students can do when given more than the usual opportunities for creative involvement.

Looking back on how we had planned our unit, I could see this sequence of steps for teaching any unit with the history workshop process:

1. Choose a topic using as criteria students' interest, teacher's interest, and materials available.
2. Determine what students know and want to know about the topic.
3. Introduce primary sources (videos, photos, primary documents), followed by History Talk Groups.
4. Introduce long-range writing assignment in some genre of historical fiction.
5. Lecture to fill in the background.
6. Continue using primary sources and History Talk Groups.
7. Continue steps in writing process: response groups and class time for writing and conferencing.
8. Schedule student presentations.

Four

Teachers at Work

During the history workshop, I kept a journal in which I recorded the exchange of questions between teachers and our students and between Linda and myself. We searched for the most effective ways to proceed. I include some of these exchanges in my story, for they seem to represent the essence of the history workshop process.

Initially, Linda and I thought that we were experimenting with a new methodology: a new combination of instructional strategies that could transform how history is taught and learned. In this process, we discovered again that methodology is not the key factor in classrooms. The key lies in the teachers' attitude toward the students; methodology helps only in so far as it shifts that attitude toward trust.

Linda and I differed in trusting our students. Initially, I was able to risk more than Linda was. Perhaps this was simply because I hadn't taught high school for twenty years and was not mired in the old paradigm of mistrust. Our co-teaching revealed the many ways that we didn't trust our students as much as we thought we did. Now we understand that our project included efforts to let go of our old attitudes of mistrust and to find classroom strategies that give responsibility to students.

On day one I introduced myself to the students, explaining why I was there, our experiment with new methods, and asked, "Do you have any questions?" I was asked if I was a psychologist; then, "What if the new methods don't work and we don't learn?" I answered that we could change our methods as we go along; it was the students' responsibility to let us know if things weren't working.

Next I introduced the project, describing what would be different for them: two teachers; no text; primary sources; more time to learn;

29

time to write stories instead of research papers; no right answers to many questions; finding answers to their own questions. I explained that they would be graded on journals and class notes, two fact and map quizzes, their story, and their presentations. Nothing else. One student asked, "Then we don't have to write out the questions and look up the answers?" "That's correct," I answered.

After this brief introduction to the course, I drew a Swastika and asked what it was. Most of them knew the name—the girl from India knew it was Sanskrit. They associated it with hate, fear, prejudice, war—I accepted all answers. Then we pursued their answers: What war? When? Who were the participants? Hate against whom? Who are Jews? People who practice a religion. Who else? Those who grew up in Jewish families but don't practice anymore. How many Jews in this class? One. How many in the United States? Someone had written a report on Judaism and knew the answer—10 million out of a population of 250 million, equals 4 percent, the same proportion as in our class. The class had guessed 10 percent. Some thought this figure too high, some too low. Can you tell Jews by their names? One student gave as an example, "Goodman." But most students weren't confident about this; they didn't realize that many names we think of as Jewish are German. They said their mothers thought they could tell Jewish names. Name some famous Jewish people, I said. They named Dianne Feinstein, Albert Einstein, Sammy Davis, Jr. (He's a convert, says Linda.) Are Jews a race? No, they said, they are all kinds of people, from many places.

What would you like to know about Nazism? I asked. Students wanted to know the number of Jews in the United States; why Nazis were prejudiced against Jews rather than other people; how Hitler survived when he contradicted his own ideals, i.e. he was dark and short instead of tall and blond; what kind of a person Hitler was; how the Nazi government operated; and how the German camps compared to U.S. concentration camps.

Overhearing one student comment, "I don't want to write about Nazism; it's too depressing," I asked, "What questions do you have about the things that are depressing?" Some wanted to know why the Nazis tortured the Jews instead of just keeping them in camps; why so few people knew about the concentration camps; if world leaders knew; why so many people followed Hitler; and if Hitler had a special propaganda leader.

Everyone was involved in the discussion; students paid rapt attention for the whole period. I responded with comments like, "That's a good (or key) question"; "that's really thinking"; "there's no right answer about this." A few times some students started to try to answer the questions and I reminded them that we wouldn't answer now but would use our questions as a guide to our study. Their first assignment included five vocabulary words: genocide, holocaust anti-Semitism, scapegoat, and stereotype. They were to find the meanings in the dictionary, the text, or ask people.

Linda was delighted with this lesson; she wanted to try it with her other classes. Until now she had been too scared to proceed as slowly as I had, she said, afraid that she would lose students' attention. But she agreed that, in this first class, they had given full attention. At one point two boys held a private conversation, but they soon rejoined the class. Linda and I discussed the method I used to keep students involved. Focusing on important ideas and linking the questions to their real lives seemed the keys to keeping the class on the topic.

Linda enjoyed day one so much that she decided to repeat it with her other history classes. In doing so she committed herself to trying history workshop on her own.

On day two we established the routine of "quick-writes," or journal writing for the first ten minutes of class. Linda had used this method in previous classes to keep students busy while she completed roll and other paper work. The first week we suggested the following topics for quick-writes:

1. What do you know about Nazism and what would you like to know?

2. Complete these sentences with stereotypic statements you have heard:

   Teachers are. . . .   Black people are. . .
   Fat people are. . .   White people are. . .
   Blondes are. . .   Nazis are. . .
   Jews are. . .

3. What is the definition of race as it pertains to human beings? What have you been taught? Does it differ from what you experience or see?

4. Why do you think people supported Hitler to the point that he became their ruler?

All of these worked well; students wrote fluently and enjoyed having the journal writing integrated with class work.

The first week proved full. On the second day we discussed the meaning of stereotypes, using students' responses to journal topic number two above and the other key concepts given in Monday's homework: genocide, holocaust, anti-Semitism, and scapegoat. These ideas provided the framework on which we would erect the rest of our unit.

We introduced the first primary documents for in-class reading on days two and three. The first reading discussed race, a concept that had to be studied before our students could make any sense of Nazism. For the reading we chose the following passage by Allen Stoskopf, from his article: "Examining Historical Roots of Racism and Anti-Semitism."

[In the early thirties] a popular book, *The Races of Man*, was being read in some of the universities and secondary schools of the United States. The author, Dr. Robert Bennet Bean, was a Professor of Anatomy at the University of Virginia. Bean had been writing magazine pieces and scholarly articles on the topic of race for more than 20 years. This short primer purported to show the essential differences between what he believed were the three basic racial types in the world. In one of the last chapters of the book he wrote.

Mental Characteristics of the Three Races

In general, the brain of the White Race is large, the convolutions are rich, with deep fissures. The mental characteristics are activity, nervous and physical vivacity, strong ambitions and passions, and high developed idealism . . .

The brain of the Yellow-Brown Race is about medium human size, with medium to good convolutions, which are sometimes varied and deep. The mental characteristics of the Yellow-Browns need further study, but they seem to be less vivacious, with emotions and passions less evident than in the other two races. They possess moderate idealism and some love of sport, but have less spirit for exploration and adventure than the White Race.

The size of the brain in the Black Race is below the medium both of the Whites and the Yellow-Browns, frequently with relatively more simple convolutions . . . The psychic activities of the Black Race are a careless, jolly vivacity, emotions and passions of short duration, and a strong and somewhat irrational egoism. Idealism, ambition, and the co-operative faculties are weak. They love amusement and sport, but have little initiative and adventurous spirit . . . They have poetry of a low order, are rather free from lasting worries, are cursed with superstitious fears and have much emotionalism in religion (1932, pp. 94–95).

By the time readers got to these conclusions, they would have already seen scores of visual images, photographs, charts, and illustrations which visually drove home Bean's essential points.

The examples just cited illustrate how racist and antisemitic ideas could be passed off as respectable science and a topic worthy of being taught in schools and universities.

We asked the class to work in groups of six, choose one student as a facilitator and one as recorder, with the other four doing most of the talking. We asked them to read the selection and talk about it, focusing on these questions:

1. Who wrote this passage?
2. If you have ever heard these ideas before, describe when and where.
3. What do you think about this passage?

Allowing five minutes for reading and about fifteen minutes for talking, we then reconvened the class and asked each recorder to report the results of his or her group discussion and then held a whole-class discussion of race.

The following is a transcript of the discussion that took place in one History Talk Group, a much more honest and intimate one than what ensued in the whole-class discussion.

Judy: Who wrote this passage?

Marlene: Dr. Bennett, no Dr. Bean. [no identification of who he was]

Judy: If you've ever heard these ideas before . . . ?

Kristin: This is what the Nazis motive was. It's just telling about what they thought. What they are saying is that the white race is like, superior, at least mentally, and stuff.

Judy: What do you think about this passage?

Melvin: It's just telling about what they [the Nazis] thought.

Marlene: I guess it is based on some research.

Melvin: In other words, the guy is prejudiced. Whites have bigger brains than blacks. If you're black, you're not smart. If you're white, you're smart.

Judy: So you guys don't really think the guy who wrote it is a Nazi?

Doug: Definitely. He's looking for Aryans. He wrote a story for Aryans, so he's gotta be. He's probably an Aryan himself.

Marlene: Then why is he saying . . . ?

Doug: He's so interested in finding a perfect Aryan.

Judy: Have you ever heard these ideas before?

Jack: Nope, never heard them.

Melvin: I have. In eighth grade in Mr. K's history class.

Doug: Ms. G. was talking about how whites are superior before class.

Kristin: I've heard it, I think, in history books actually. I think that history books kind of give that idea. I'm totally serious, because you know how they totally talk about the slave trade. They're always putting it from a white person's point of view.

Marlene: Yeah, I've heard it before a lot.

On day four we showed the video, *Hitler: A Study of a Tyranny*, and on day five I introduced writing by asking students what kind of writing they usually did in history class. None, they said. Eventually some remembered that they write journals regularly, and they thought of the research paper that they will do next year. I described research papers and reports and essays as being expository writing, characterized by having a main idea that you develop, support with evidence, and answer possible criticisms. I then suggested a whole different kind of writing—stories, or narratives. The students thought of short stories, plays, and novels. I described the basic characteristics to include characters, setting, plot with conflict, and resolution. Then I described biography and autobiography, both non-fictional and fictional ones. I told the class that we wanted them to write fictional biography. We talked about what that was and that it needed to have a real historical setting in Europe in the 1930s and 1940s.

We expected students to protest that they didn't know how to write stories. Instead they surprised us.

Ms. Brown: Make up a person that you'd like to be during the time of Hitler and the Holocaust and decide where that person is going to live and be. So you have to create the setting, and then you make up a story about what happens to that person.

Student: Does it have to be about somebody who really was in that time or do you just make up names?

Ms. Brown: You're right. It's the second. You make it up, but you write all the details as accurately as you can for the history of that time. So you can't put them on another planet or somewhere else. You put them somewhere in Germany, and you try to get the details as accurate as you possibly can. It doesn't have to be Germany. It could be anywhere in Europe.

Student: Does it have to be someone you'd like to be, I mean, that's kind of hard because nobody had a good life then.

Ms. Brown: You don't have to pick this person for two more weeks, so you'll have two weeks to think about it. You'll be learning lots more about all the possible kinds of people you could choose. But you're asking a good question, that is, you may choose somebody whose life is not that pleasant.

Ms. Danielson: It isn't necessary that you do, but you could just be someone who was lucky, but the things you witness, maybe torment you inside. Nobody could have been perfectly happy and know what's going on.

Student: That's what I mean.

Since we didn't know whether our students had any experience writing stories, we believed that we should model their assignment. Linda and I carried on a conversation in front of the class about how we were thinking about the characters we wanted to write about.

Linda wanted to be a non-Jewish, single mother of three daughters, who has Jewish friends and has to decide whether or not to help them after she becomes aware of what is going on. She has to decide what town to live in; she wants to be near some concentration camp.

I wanted to be a teacher who is told to teach Nazi racist theories as part of my curriculum, and I want to figure out a way to resist. The librarian at Novato told me about a resistance group called the White Rose, so I want to try to find out where that group was located before I decide where to put my fictional self.

Linda perceptively remarked that she and I want to be who we are since our identity is so fixed that we have difficulty imagining ourselves as anyone else. But our students, without a fixed identity of long duration, seem more able to imagine themselves as anybody.

Immediately, several of the boys wanted to be Hitler. Linda said that it's acceptable to be a good guy or a bad guy, but maybe they would want to be an assistant to Hitler rather than Hitler himself, since Hitler was a real person. One girl thought out loud about being someone who cleaned out the death chambers.

We suggested that one way to get ideas is to read, and passed out the bibliography of books for extra credit. Linda described the *Maus* books, and I told about *The Cage* and *Night*. Students were full of interest; two books were checked out, and several said they had to wait until after final exams or they would read all weekend.

We finished day five by passing out a collection called "The Nazi Holocaust," consisting of photographs that were 11 inches by 14 inches mounted on posterboard that our librarian found in a nearby school library. Each student got one, and they could exchange with a neighbor after they finished looking. They were full of questions and comments. Certainly the photos brought a reality to our study that nothing else had. We decided to put them up around the room.

During the discussion of photos I introduced the fact that the Nazis wanted to cleanse what they called the Aryan race by eliminating any group considered as misfit. Nazis killed Gypsies, now called the Romany people; dissenters; Jehovah's Witnesses; and homosexuals. The mention of this last group prompted giggles, which I ignored, because I knew we were going to deal head-on with this later. Linda described who Gypsies were and why they were easy to scapegoat: they were nomadic, had no formal education, were not Christian. I described the symbols each group had to wear (yellow stars for Jews, pink triangles for homosexuals, brown triangles for Gypsies, and purple triangles for Jehovah's Witnesses). The students gave rapt attention until the bell rang. We gave no assignment except to prepare for finals, which would interrupt our unit for one week.

Linda and I both felt very pleased with how the first week went; she started thinking about how to teach other units this way. Her other history classes went as well as ours did, with the level of interest much higher than usual, she felt.

To make all the necessary decisions, we consulted with each other in class as we went along, and the students got to see us thinking about what to do next. We were modeling how teachers think; the students must have learned a lot about teaching.

During week two we focused almost entirely on reading and responding to primary accounts that would give our students information about Nazism and give them ideas for their story's character. We chose one primary source written by a German Catholic boy remembering what happened on his street on *Kristallnacht* (the Night of the Broken Glass), two sources by mothers who were rounded up in Jewish ghettoes and sent to camps, and one source by Rudolf Hoess, the Nazi commandant at Auschwitz. In his account, he described exactly how the poisonous showers worked. The last set of primary sources included a series of eight short descriptions of those who rescued Jews. This selection of accounts presented a full range of perspectives, which gave our students a corresponding range of roles on which to model their character.

As I had hoped, this format enabled our students to express freely their questions.

- What if there was an American Jew in Germany?
- Could kids be put in concentration camps?
- What did the Pope think?
- Who was the Pope then?
- What happened when the Jews went to Palestine?
- Did Italy surrender before Germany?
- What happened to Mussolini?
- How did the Nazis find out if someone was a homosexual?
- What if you had a Christian dad and a Jewish mom?
- What if a Jew passed a Nazi on the street; what would the encounter be like?
- Were people in the United States blaming Jews for having to fight Germany?
- How did Albania manage to stay out of being conquered—it's so small?
- What was the Gestapo?

- How big were concentration camps?
- What exactly went on in the medical experiments?
- How did Hitler die and what happened to his body?

Clearly, our students were thinking about these issues outside of history class. Linda and I wrote all of the questions on butcher paper as they surfaced. We discussed possible answers with our students. We supplied information when we could and reported back to class when we located additional facts in our reading. We didn't ask the students to research; that would punish them for asking questions, and they had enough to do. But students voluntarily shared information that they picked up from their reading. By the end of the week Linda exclaimed, "Well, it really feels as if we are all learning together."

As an example of this, the most voracious reader in the class, Sangeeta, told the class that Hitler did have a minister of propaganda; Hitler didn't do that part all himself. Linda read a book suggesting that Hitler did not have a personal hatred against Jews—at least not in the beginning—but that he took advantage of anti-Semitism in southern Germany as a tool to gain support for his fledgling party. Sangeeta read the same book, and they discussed whether or not they agreed with this interpretation. Not every student was able to carry on this kind of conversation, but they all heard it.

Most of class time was devoted to reading documents, discussing them in History Talk Groups, and reporting the results back to the class for whole group discussion. We also talked abut the writing assignment (one journal topic was to write about the decision you have made about your character), and we gave a few short mini-lectures. Both Linda and I felt strongly that the basic facts and chronology had to be learned. Perhaps this was an issue of cultural literacy, but we wanted our students to know certain fundamental information to construct meaning and to be prepared for tests and more learning in the future.

During one class Linda passed out a worksheet—a chronology that included key facts and space for notes—as she reviewed events leading to Kristallnacht. The next day she described ghetto life, and I discussed the armed resistance in the Warsaw Ghetto. We went over two maps, one showing the number and percentage of Jews in each European country, and the other showing the location of the major concentration camps, both labor and death camps.

Linda created a worksheet to help students get started with their writing. She titled it "Getting Started—Plot Sketch." Linda included the following questions on the worksheet and left enough space for answers:

Getting Started—Plot Sketch

1. What is your character's full name?
2. Are you going to tell the story in the first or third person?
3. Briefly describe your character's appearance at the time the story takes place. Consider facial hair, facial features, coloring, height, weight, clothing, etc.
4. What nationality and/or religion is your character?
5. What languages does she/he speak?
6. Will your character be communicating with someone whose native tongue is different from his or her own? Why or why not?
7. Is it necessary for your character to speak more than one language? Why or why not?
8. How old is your character at the time the events of your story occur?
9. In what year do the events of the story take place?
10. How old is he/she when they get around to telling the story? Is the story told as a memory of the past?
11. What particular historical event(s) will your story describe?
12. Where exactly will your story take place (use real names)? Will some scenes be in one location and others in another location? Why?
13. Why did you choose this particular time and place?
14. What role will your character have in the events you describe— will she/he be a Jew, a Nazi, a rescuer, a silent witness, etc.?
15. Why did you decide to make your character that way?
16. What problem or conflict will your character have to deal with?
17. Will he or she finally overcome or solve the problem? Why or why not?
18. Briefly describe the scene in which the conflict is resolved for good or for bad. How many people are involved? Where does it occur? Describe the scene as though you are a witness.
19. Your story can be told in many different ways. You can tell it in straight chronological order, or you can use flashbacks. You can tell your story through diary or journal entries. How do you think you will tell your story?
20. What scene will you illustrate in your drawing? Why that particular scene?
21. Draw a story board or flow chart to show the sequence of your story's events.

Linda gave the students two days to complete the worksheet and then collected them. We graded them during class so that students could have their worksheet to help them write their first draft over the weekend. While they were talking in groups, we simply counted the number of categories to which they had given some response and graded accordingly. For example, those who gave any response to nineteen questions or more got an A. I was not happy with this mode of evaluation, but Linda felt that it helps students stay "on track." Without it, she believed, many would procrastinate and be unable to produce a first draft within a few days. But some students could fill in the form only *after* they had written their story. In my opinion, the worksheet had too many questions and the students should feel free to choose whatever exercise helped them get started—drawing a picture, writing a description of their character, or anything else. If our students had some experience with this kind of project before, perhaps we would have had more confidence that they would find their own way to begin.

By the end of week two Linda and I were having a fine time. We did, however, have a sense of rushing and of making hasty decisions about grading, about the sequence of events. Linda was amazed at how much there was to do and how different it felt from her usual teaching, where the teacher is always trying to think up the next activity. I expected this to happen. With history workshop each activity seems to generate more, and there's never enough time. Teaching becomes primarily deciding what to leave out.

During the third week we used the whole range of teaching procedures—two days of lectures, one day of History Talk Groups, one day of writing groups, and one day of testing. Linda lectured about the events leading up to World War II and the war itself. By this time the students seemed hungry for the information. They were full of questions: Were all Germans expected to join the army? Did the age range for soldiers decrease when they started losing? What does D stand for in D-Day? Did the Allies test the A-bomb anywhere? Why didn't the United States drop an A-bomb on Vietnam?

Twelve days into our unit we collected the first draft of their stories. Linda had already collected them from her first period class. She remarked, "I am really pleased with their stories. I think they *liked* doing it." We received confirming feedback from the campus supervisor who told Linda in the copy room: "Oh, I've heard about your assignment. The kids are talking all over the campus about their stories."

During the third week, we dealt with the issue of how homosexuals were persecuted by Nazis. I began the discussion by acknowledging that the issue of homosexuality is controversial, and that it was also a source of diverse opinions in Hitler's time. I knew the students probably had strong and different opinions, which I wanted them to express. I indicated that differing opinions were fine, but I didn't want to hear any insults or put-downs that might offend homosexual persons if they heard them. I went right on to describe "The Night of the Long Knives" when Hitler had the chief of the S.A. (Sturmabteilung, storm troopers or Brownshirts) shot because he was openly homosexual. A few lessons back one of our students had raised the question, "How did the Nazis know who was gay?" My answer included reading parts of a letter written in September, 1935, by a young gay German about what was happening to his friend, who had escaped to Switzerland (Plant, 1986). The Nazis raided gay bars, forced gays to tell about their friends, and confiscated address books. Our students were spellbound.

Linda and I distributed a general description of Nazi ideology and laws about homosexuals and their treatment in concentration camps, the draft for a new edition of *Facing History and Ourselves* (in press, 1994). Students read the document for ten minutes then discussed it in History Reading Groups for fifteen minutes. Linda structured the discussion so that the group reporter wrote down each student's response and then added the general conclusion of the group. This kept groups on task; we collected the reports, but there was no time for oral reports to the whole class. The students discussed the topic with no giggling or rude comments; they certainly rose to the occasion and seemed pleased to be given mature material.

The next day we began with a report from the History Talk Groups about their previous discussion of Nazi treatment of homosexuals. Group reporters had turned in their written notes and were eager for our response: our acknowledgment that they had dealt responsibly with this controversial issue. Linda and I assured them of our satisfaction, and the reporters gave fine oral reports. This is a sample of their written notes:

M: It was interesting that Hitler allowed homosexuals high in his staff.

J: Thought it intriguing that women weren't arrested.

C: Thought this was disgusting.

Group: This was very informative.

From their reports and from our tapes, we knew that the History Talk Groups gave our students a more intimate level of discourse than usually is achieved in history class. The following discussion that took place in one History Talk Group reveals their spontaneous and candid opinions:

So what do you think?

Homophobia.

Nosey, they're just nosey.

Eventually if they say homosexuality was wrong, I don't think they had any right to totally torture people because of it.

I think they were just—they had this weird fear that they would ruin their society.

Yeah.

That's just like what they had with the Jews.

And all the other groups they put in concentration camps.

I think they were just nosey. If they had just minded their own business, it would have never happened.

Sure. (sarcastically)

Still, I think it was really weird to think how long it's taken to be able to be sexual or anything like that.

Yeah, we're so used to—We've all lived here. All of their other laws were totally screwed up anyway, so it's kind of weird to be all kind of totally free here, be able to do whatever you want, and then hear stories about somewhere else where you can't.

I mean, there's a lot of pressure here, too.

Cause I mean I think homosexuality—Personally, I think it's wrong, but I don't think people should be tortured or should be made fun of because they are.

Personally, I don't care. It doesn't concern me. If I'm not homosexual, then why should I care who is? They are still people, and they don't deserve to be tortured. Just because they're different, there's no reason for . . .

That's true. Actually . . . (giggles)

Let's see what else they say (refers to document): "Whoever thinks of homosexual love is our enemy, emasculates our people."

Okay.

I think Hitler didn't have all his screws tight in his head, right?

He just obviously thought these people were going to ruin their perfect society, or something.

And he was the one who was ruining their society in the first place.

At the end of the third week of the workshop, we conducted our first Writing Response Group. As far as we knew, most of our students had never done this before. Linda had prepared a form for them called "Student Evaluation of Student Writing." It had five questions/statements with lots of space between them:

1. What is the story about?

2. What do you like best about the story?

3. What do you dislike or find confusing about the story?

4. Ask specific questions you have about specific aspects of the story.

5. Make one or two suggestions that will help the writer revise his or her paper.

Linda gave instructions for using the form: each reader would respond to each question; there was room for three responses under each question if there was enough time to read the stories written by the other members of their group. She also explained what they needed to do for their second draft—respond to the comments they received, finish the story, and get the historical information as accurate as possible.

The groups got underway, and students were absorbed in their work the rest of the period. Five students had not yet turned in a first draft; we decided they couldn't participate in their groups, since it would mean that someone wouldn't have a story to read. We asked them to work individually at their desks and get their story started, giving us a chance to conference with them one-on-one. This worked fine. I talked with Joan, who asked "How do I start?" I asked her if she had picked a character yet and she responded, "Well, maybe a Jew." I asked, "Who do you sympathize with as we talk about the Holocaust?" "The children," replied Joan. "So maybe you could be a Jewish girl in a large family who has several younger children to take care of," I suggested. This was all she needed; Joan spent the rest of the period writing, only raising her hand to ask for help in thinking of a Polish name.

Alison, who is used to making good grades, had no draft and didn't want to start writing. She hung around the nearest group, reading over their shoulders and listening to their conversations. Before the class departed she managed to borrow several stories to read; she was learning how to do it from her classmates. I guessed that she was afraid to try something new, afraid of not being able to make an A on her first attempt.

I observed to several writers of the more accomplished stories, "I bet you may have trouble revising. Your stories are nearly perfect already." "Not at all," laughed Sangeeta, "I have lots of ideas about what to do to make it better."

During cleanup some students were still reading; for homework, we asked the students to find one more person—a parent, friend, sibling—to read and write comments on their story. We didn't see the comment sheets then; they were returned to the writer, who needed it for working on revisions due in five days. Linda and I asked students to include the comment sheet with their second draft. We wouldn't know until then what kind of suggestions they were able to make to each other.

On Friday Linda gave a test; I missed the first half of class to supervise one of my student teachers. Linda often writes her own tests, but this time she used the one from the textbook to save time and to reassure herself that we were covering the curriculum. The test was multiple choice and covered information that Linda had given the class in two lectures during the week. Most students made high grades—90s and 100s—on it. During the time remaining after the test, which took about fifteen minutes, we went through the questions raised by students, written on charts hanging over the blackboard. We only got through question six, reviewing the answers we and they had discovered and discussing them further. Linda and I marked where we stopped on the chart, promising to pick up again when we had time.

Week four began with a holiday. When classes resumed, we conducted a writing clinic, my favorite aspect of the project. I had realized over the weekend that we were still being too directive and were too much in control. We hadn't yet given our students a period in which they could decide what they needed to do next. They still didn't have real ownership of their work, at least not in class.

I came to class fifteen minutes early and told Linda that I wanted today to be a writing clinic in which each student could decide what to do. Linda expressed reluctance. She feared there would be lots of talking and not much working. When I suggested that one of their options would be to conference with one of us, she feared they would all rush up to our desk or hold their hands up waiting for us to attend them, meanwhile doing nothing. But since Linda, too, wanted to see what would happen, she agreed.

Giving the class instructions, I said that students could choose what they wanted to do from these possibilities: continue writing on their story, correct spelling and verify information, design and draw their illustrations, share their story with a friend who would offer feedback, read their extra-credit books and write up a review, ask for a short conference with us, or ask for assistance from a friend. Options not available were working on homework from another class or not working at all.

Everyone fell right to work on a variety of tasks. Several students worked on their stories. Several drew illustrations. A few checked the spelling of words with dictionaries. Several students read and discussed with friends. One girl filled in the plot sketch that she never had done; now that she had written her story, she could do it. Another student took the test she missed Friday while I read the first draft of her story, which we discussed when she finished the test. Linda strolled around the room, occasionally being stopped by a student for a brief conference. I conferenced with a few students, but they were working so self-sufficiently that I got out my camera and began taking pictures. (I had warned them that I might start doing this.)

Class continued like this until the last five minutes, when we assigned as homework the reading of the last document, an account of liberation day in the camps. Not once during this period did we call down a student or ask for quiet or go "Shhh." Dumbfounded, Linda said to me after class, "To make it work, you just have to let go."

Before the bell we collected all the stories for the second checkpoint; we're trying not to call them drafts, since that implies a finished product. The students should be able to decide how many drafts; we just want to collect them twice before the final version. A few students worry about the number of pages, but not many. Originally, we said five to ten pages; now we just say, "However long it takes to tell your story." Gradually we are learning to let go.

In the middle of the week Linda lectured, trying to cover all the terms she wanted them to know. This didn't go as well as it had before—students felt confused and disconnected. There were probably several reasons for this. Linda was rushed and tried to get too much in; she probably included too many items and wasn't selective enough of the essential ones. Linda even included terms covering the postwar time that wasn't part of our unit. Maybe our students had already stopped thinking about terms to focus on meaning.

The next day the school secretary, Marie Benson, visited our class to talk about her experience in wartime Germany. Her father had been a German soldier, imprisoned for going slightly contrary to orders, but listed as missing in action. Her mother, left with two little girls, escaped a burning building after their village was bombed. They survived by resettlement in a rural place with a farm family, who were forced by the government to take refugees from other areas of the country. When she was seventeen and working in a bar, Marie fell in love with an American soldier. Eventually she married him and came to this country, where they have been together happily for thirty-one years. Marie was honest about the pain of her German experience; we hung on every word. Students asked probing questions, like "Did you have any Jewish friends?"

At the end of the week we collected the illustrations for the stories. Almost everyone had them, although the girls seemed much shyer about drawing than the boys. Linda and I talked about several ways we could have made this assignment more effective. Perhaps if the students drew the illustrations before starting to write, they could envision the details more easily. Or they could stop writing and illustrate if they became blocked and couldn't decide how to continue. Another possibility included waiting until the end after they figured out the most gripping scene. As soon as someone made a drawing it could be exhibited, which might act as a spur to others. Students will want to do the work if they have a chance to share and to make decisions themselves; in the unusual case where a student does not produce some work, then the teacher would have the opportunity to find out what was going on. I agreed with Linda on her suggestion that students be asked to provide captions to their illustrations.

Linda returned the "second drafts"; I didn't have a chance to read them. She was overwhelmed with reading them, setting her alarm at five A.M. to get through them all. It was simply not realistic to collect the stories so often. Of course, she couldn't read them closely, and many students felt their grade was not justified. Apparently, Linda felt that she had graded leniently the first time and now needed to tighten up. Many students received a lower grade on this second draft than on the first, and they wanted an explanation. Ruth, who is usually an A student, got a B+ on her second draft. Linda explained that the historical dates and information came at the end of the story and they should have been at the beginning. After several moments of somewhat heated discussion, I jumped in to re-state Linda's position. She had been saying, "I think that your story is better if the information comes first." I re-stated this as: "In Mrs. Danielson's judgment, your story would be more effective if the historical information came at the beginning." "In that case," responded the student, "I will have to take a lower grade, because in my judgment it is more effective at the end." "Well," I thought, "Now we're getting somewhere."

This incident is important. By changing two words in Linda's response, it became possible for Ruth to take ownership of her piece. As long as Linda said, "I think," she was exerting her authority as teacher, and the student couldn't disagree without defying her. But when Linda's opinion was stated as her *judgment*, then the student could counterpose her own. The word *better* has such overtones of moral superiority that it is difficult to disagree. The word *effective* is morally neutral and allows disagreement. Does the effectiveness of our teaching hang on our choice of words? It seems likely.

By this time the contradiction between our grading policy and our methodology was apparent to us. We tried to give ownership to students, but we still graded them at each little step of the way by some criteria unknown to them and not too clear to us. Linda and I were knee-deep in a double message that could undermine our whole project. By week four I realized that we shouldn't be grading successive drafts; students should simply receive feedback from their peers and from us. Our grading policy continued Linda's usual practice, which she believed was necessary to keep students working. Now she, too, saw that in history workshop students didn't need the threat of grades to keep working.

The final two weeks of our project were filled with collecting final drafts of stories, watching a video, listening to students tell their stories to their classmates, and evaluating our project with our students.

When we began the video, The Wave, our students were mesmerized. Since time ran out, we had to postpone the ending until the next day—an effective strategy. The students begged for it from the moment they entered the classroom. Our dialogue afterwards proved disappointing, but we were all too moved to talk much. Most of the more vocal students believe that imposing a comprehensive ideology couldn't happen here; Americans wouldn't go for that much loss of freedom and self-choice. In the film the student who most enjoyed belonging to The Wave was Robert, who was an outsider, teased by other students. One of our students asked why Robert was so upset to discover that The Wave was a hoax. Our student still didn't grasp the security that a group ideology offered its members.

Before we finished the video we collected the final drafts of stories—an exciting moment for everyone. Linda and I asked for all drafts, the plot sketch, the feedback sheets—everything they had used as they worked on their stories. I could hardly wait to read the stories, and the students' pride was evident in the pleasure they took from turning in a finished product.

Linda and I had made a schedule for each student to have five minutes to present their story. We gave instructions that each student was to tell their story or tell about it, but not read it. The presentations had to include interesting story-word pictures, delivery (eye contact, gestures, enthusiasm), and a maximum five-minute delivery.

When the student began their presentations, Linda and I relaxed to the pleasure of hearing students talk about their stories. However, without prompts from us they finished too quickly! Most students didn't go into enough detail about their reasons for writing this story, and several rushed through. Some gave a detailed analysis of what the story concerned. We asked a few questions of those who finished quickly. Both Linda and I encouraged the class to ask questions but they were reluctant. I wished we had built that into the expectations.

Most of the next class consisted of more presentations, which, again, took less time than we wished. The last fifteen minutes of class we discussed other genocides. I led the discussion and taped it, trying hard to formulate effective questions and keep my own opinions out. Students were fascinated and contributed what they knew; Erik was able to describe the Cambodian genocide conducted by the Khmer Rouge. I explained the Armenian and Tibetan exterminations and questioned whether the deaths of Native Americans after Europeans settled in North America and the deaths of millions of Africans on the passage from Africa to the Caribbean and the Americas constituted genocides. The whole class considered the meaning of genocide, what it included and what it didn't and arrived at some clarity. These whole-class discussions are an important element in history workshop; we teachers need to be highly skilled at conducting them for maximum content and clarity, especially in a workshop format where they play a subsidiary role.

During the final week more students presented their stories. All of them did well, but many complained that they didn't enjoy making oral presentations. Fear of public speaking seems to run very deep, even in an informal, friendly atmosphere. We keep thinking, of course, that students' fear will diminish with practice.

Linda guided the presentations on these two days, while I worked in the library interviewing individual students about their stories. I led the closure and evaluation of the unit, and during the last two classes, our students watched the video *The Hiding Place*, about Dutch Protestants who hid Jews. A substitute teacher managed the class, since Linda was at a conference in San Diego and I continued to interview students individually. During the final two weeks I managed a total of ten interviews, lasting about twenty minutes each.

Throughout history workshop, Linda and I collected journals every two weeks and gave a map and fact test on most Fridays. The story and its presentation accounted for the rest of the unit's grade with extra credit for book reports. The first draft of the story was worth two-hundred points, judged solely on the creation of the storyline. The second draft was worth two-hundred points, judged for historical information and accuracy. The final draft was worth three-hundred points, judged by both criteria above and mechanics (spelling, grammar, and punctuation). The presentation was worth two-hundred points, evaluated on its interest, delivery (eye contact, gestures, enthusiasm), and five-minute time limit.

Even though we told students at the beginning of the workshop that we both would grade their work, Linda did most of the grading. I was overwhelmed with documenting the project and too uncertain how to be consistent with her standards. Doing it together would have required far more time than proved feasible.

On the final stories Linda broke the grade into two parts, mechanics and story, and averaged for the total grade. This enabled her to reward students for good stories despite difficulty with spelling and punctuation. Linda deducted twenty points if there was no preface. Although she gave no points for the illustration, everyone turned one in!

Looking at points for the total unit, the journals counted for three hundred points, the tests for two hundred points, the story a total of seven hundred points, and its presentation was worth two hundred points. Each extra book report counted one hundred points. Grades for the unit fell into this distribution: nine As, eight Bs, five Cs, and two Ds. These grades seemed to Linda somewhat higher than usual.

Linda and I finished exhausted, but satisfied. The final two weeks of presentations had given us and our students a chance to wind down from the intensity of the first four weeks. We would need some distance before we could dispassionately evaluate what had happened. But we had seen our students' pride in their stories, and we knew that we had never before experienced such excitement in teaching. Our most difficult issue had been learning to let go of our control, but our students taught us. Whenever we managed to open up decision making to them, they rewarded our trust. Both of us finished feeling that we could never go back to our old ways.

Five

Students and Their Stories

Our class of twenty-five students chose a wide range of characters on which to base their stories. When students explained their choices, many said they felt that most of the class chose one character-type—Jewish. Because of this feeling, some wanted to try something different and chose a Nazi character. The distribution of character choice turned out about even across three categories: eight students chose Jewish victims, eight chose German non-Nazis who resisted Hitler's regime, and six chose Nazi characters, some of whom changed their minds about Nazism and some of whom did not. Three students chose as main characters persons outside of Germany—a U.S. prisoner of war, and two Danes who rescued Jews.

To discover if gender made any difference in the telling of the stories, I analyzed the girls' stories separately from the boys'. The class included eleven boys, five of whom were making Ds and one an A when our unit began. With fourteen girls in the class, eight were making As, with no Ds. This may be typical of history classes, but why?

Of the fourteen girls in the class, six chose Jews as their story's subject; five chose Germans married to Jews, German rescuers of Jews, or German resisters of Nazi propaganda; two chose Danes who rescued Jews; and one chose a German woman who discovers that her mother was Jewish and renounces Nazism, even though her husband is a Nazi.

All students chose a character of their own gender except two girls who chose to be men, and Ruth, who developed her plot around two main characters, one an adult male and the other a teenage girl, as seen in her story included in my opening chapter.

Ruth is a young woman of astonishing beauty—serene, rosy face, with thick, black hair almost to her waist. Sitting in the front row in one of the seats nearest the teacher's desk, she stands out at once as an eager student accustomed to the As that Linda assured me she always earns.

But Ruth never speaks during class discussions. She listens intently, but something about her keeps her from jumping into the verbal fray. She looks Asian, but not fully. She speaks with no trace of an accent.

My conference with Ruth revealed that her mother was full Chinese, her father English-American. She is the youngest of five children. Her mother died when Ruth was five years old. Her father raised all his children as a single parent, earning his living as an artist who sells his paintings through galleries. Ruth is glad that she is the last, because she would be jealous if there were a younger sibling, even though she says that her father acts with great fairness toward all. Her older sister is at Columbia University, one brother is at University of Arizona, and her other sister attends Wellesley.

Ruth said that her main character started out to be Sarah Rothschild, a French-Jewish teenager who fought to the end in the Warsaw Ghetto. But as Ruth wrote about the person who helped Sarah and her family, she got so deep into that person, Jan Karski, that she had to have two main characters. "It's just the way it turned out," she says.

To start her story, Ruth borrowed a book from the public library about the Warsaw Ghetto. It had pictures and facts about the major episodes, which helped Ruth greatly. She also talked to her father, who gave her ideas about the kinds of guns and ammunition the Jews used. Ruth's father loves history and helps her with all her assignments.

Ruth wants to be a writer when she grows up. She came to this decision in elementary school. She just likes writing stories and does it for fun, not only for assignments. Ruth trusts that her stories will flow when she is ready to write them.

For this assignment Ruth waited until the night before the first draft was due. When she started writing, her ideas flowed as fast as she could type. She didn't think about whether the narrative should be in the first person or the third person; she just wrote. Ruth didn't think her story would be as long as it turned out to be, but when she finished the main part, she wanted to write in diary form to show the feelings of someone actually fighting in the ghetto.

Ruth decided to put dates in her preface and at the end of her story. Linda graded her down on her second draft, suggesting that the dates should come in the beginning of the story to help orient her readers. In a talk with us after class, Ruth resisted that suggestion, but eventually she accepted it. "She [Mrs. Danielson] wanted dates in the beginning. I revised it to put some dates in the beginning. I did it to please her. I didn't want to be marked down for something that she wanted. I guess it did make more sense if the date was in the beginning."

Ruth was surprised that few other students created characters across gender lines. For her, it just seemed natural. She felt that since, historically, a lot of women helped the Jews get out of the Warsaw ghetto, and a lot of men did, too, her story was just the way it should be.

When I asked Ruth why she chose Sarah as the main character instead of her brother, Joshua, she replied:

> I think it was because I envisioned myself fighting in the ghetto. It seemed easier because I am a girl, and she would be a girl, so it just seemed the way it should be. I just thought of anyone fighting for their freedom. All those stories about slavery and everything just came to me, and I just wrote them down. Also, there is so much sexism going on, like women aren't as capable as men. And my story showed that women are capable, or even more capable, than some men. So that's the way I did it. So I am in the story, sort of.
>
> I'm in the character of Jan, too, sort of. I guess I help a lot of people who are less fortunate. At Christmas time I always give my change to the Salvation Army when the people ring the bells. It's just what I would do if I was in that situation. I'd fight for what I believe, and that's my feelings for that character.
>
> I don't know whether I could write a story about a Nazi character. It's hard for me to think of all the hate they must have to be like that towards Jews. I've never really hated someone, so I don't think I could. I have to feel what my character's going to feel.

Ruth didn't notice our process of teaching as it happened. When we talked afterwards, she realized that it must have consisted of "personal documents, conversations, and opinions." She thought that the History Talk Groups didn't work, that everyone just goofed around. She likes textbooks in general and read hers at home for this unit. In addition to the text, she felt she learned most from the personal opinions of her classmates.

Ruth certainly fulfilled all my expectations about how teenagers think about history. She put herself in the historical situation, explored her own character and gender, and defined herself as one who would fight for her convictions. She thought and wrote from feelings as well as from logic and chronology. She felt somewhat insecure, since she was used to learning from textbooks, but she excelled in historical thinking.

Ruth's story illustrates my claim that teenagers are busy forming their conscious identity and that studying history can be a powerful avenue for defining themselves. In her story Ruth tried on two possible identities: an adult who rescued victims of his government and a teenager who fought to death to resist victimization. Through her imagination Ruth planned how she might act in the future if ever faced with such a situation and increased the chance that she will be able to resist group pressures to conform. Ruth saw that her values derived from her father's values; she didn't seem to explore what her mother's Chinese culture may mean to her.

As a teacher, I want to help teenagers create powerful identities. If they can become aware of who they are and what their family and culture mean, then they can emerge from these years with enough confidence to assume productive adult roles or enough resolve to change who they are. People who give little thought to their identity seem less able to take charge of their lives. Ruth seems to be ready for whatever comes.

Behind Ruth sat Sangeeta, a small, dark, young woman who looked as if she might be from India. One of those eager students whose eyes always meet the teacher's, Sangeeta wrote this story:

Realizations

"Ellen!" I called to my friend in the distance.

She turned, cheerfully calling back, "Hi, Nina! How are you?"

"Just fine. How about you?" I replied, catching up with her. We were both the same age; seventeen, yet we were so different. She was tall with large brown eyes and shoulder-length dark hair. I, on the other hand, was very short, with long light brown hair and green eyes that everybody described as "striking." At school I was known for my inquisitive nature, while Ellen was known for her quiet studiousness. That is, when we went to the same school. "So," I said, "how's school?"

Ellen winced. I knew I shouldn't have brought it up. I just wanted for it to be as it was. We used to always talk about school and our plans for the future. She wanted, as I did, to go to the University, and study medicine, and it was all about to happen, when. . . .

"It's all right, I guess," Ellen said, interrupting my thoughts. She was clearly unhappy. "It's just that children of all ages are all in the same cramped classroom, and we never learn anything because the little kids are always screaming and it's just awful! I'm simply miserable!" she cried, throwing her arms around me. "I just wish I could go to school with you again."

"Just think, in one more year we'll graduate, and you'll be out of the Jewish school and into the University," I said, attempting to comfort her.

"The University? It seemed so possible just a few months ago. Now it all seems so far away."

"My mother will be expecting me—I should leave," I said hesitantly. Her forlorn state which was so out of character had left me worried. "Please come and visit me sometime soon."

"Nina, is that you, darling? Why are you late?" called my mother. Lately, my mother had been more concerned with my whereabouts.

"I saw Ellen, we talked for a while."

"How is she? I saw Ellen's mother today, at the market. She is very worried."

"Ellen is all right. She cannot stand the Jewish school they sent her to, though. Why is Ellen's mother worried?"

"That poor girl. She was one of the smartest in your class, wasn't she? Two months ago, our President von Hindenburg died, as you know. Hitler has taken his place. He has been named the leader."

"Oh, yes, a man came and talked to our class today. He was a member of the Nazi party. He said that Hitler was going to help make Germany a better and more powerful nation. He told us different ways we can help. First, he taught us to raise our arms and shout 'Heil Hitler.' Then, he showed us some diagrams. He showed us a diagram of a German person, one of us, and another of a Jew. He taught us that Germans are better built and more intelligent than Jews are. You know what else he said, Mama? He said that Jews are trying to make us lower, and that we should prevent that from happening."

"Enough, Nina Anne." Her voice had a strange sharpness to it. "You always believed all that they say at school, but now they are not telling the truth. Perhaps Hitler will make Germany a better place, but I will not have you believing that Jews are inferior to us. What about Ellen? Is she less intelligent than you? Is she trying to degrade you in any way? This is all nonsense that you mustn't believe, Nina."

"But Mama, maybe Ellen and her family are different. This man *taught* us this, it must be right. You always said that whatever is taught must be learnt, and that is what I am doing. He showed us proof that we are better. He had pictures and diagrams, and even a brain from one of us and a Jew. The one from the Jew was so much smaller."

"Nina, you are old enough now to think for yourself." My mother's voice was almost frighteningly quiet. "I do not need to feed ideas into your head and neither do people from your school. I am telling you once again that they are wrong. You are merely excited by his 'scientific' evidence. God made us all equal, and we must know that to be a fact, or we will not be able to live in harmony with one another. I will simply say that whenever you begin to think that these people are right, think of your friend Ellen. Think about how she is suffering in that terrible school. Think about how this may only be the beginning of further things much worse than a cramped schoolroom. Think, Nina. You must think. I will say no more about this matter." With these words of conviction, she resumed the cooking she had momentarily stopped.

The conversation drifted to other topics, but my mind remained with our discussion. Indeed, I was thinking about the matter rather deeply. On one hand, the man in school had straight out told us these things, and we had accepted them as facts. On the other hand, Mama had told me so strongly not to believe what they said about this matter. Why would the man lie, though? I had always trusted Mama, and I followed her advice, but for some reason I was torn.

What I had neglected to tell Mama was that I was considering signing up for a group called "Hitler's Youth for Girls." The man had told us all about it. We would get to participate in all sorts of activities, wear an official uniform, and best of all, we would be helping the fatherland, Germany. The man said he would be back tomorrow for signups, so we had a day to make our decision. I had thought it would be interesting to join. After all, my cousin at the University says that many professors there are more favorable to those involved with the Nazis. It sounded like a good thing to do, too, helping the fatherland. But something in what Mama had said struck me. What if this was really only the beginning—a small cramped schoolroom. Could it really be that there were worse things on the way? I had told Ellen she could trust me, and yet I am accepting that she could possibly be inferior on the basis of her heritage. I am still confused, I must think.

"Good Morning, class. Starting today, we will begin each class with the salute you learned yesterday. For those of you who have forgotten, we will do it once for practice. Ready?"

"Heil Hitler," the class said weakly.

"This time, anybody who does not say it with full force will receive ten lashes. Now," he said, throwing up his arm in full salute.

"HEIL HITLER!" the words resounded in the room.

"Now, I am passing around a sheet for those who are interested in Hitler's Youth for Girls. Please sign your name in the upper left column . . ." I was oblivious to what the teacher was saying, as I was still in shock at what had just happened. Who was Hitler? Was he not a person, after all? Just as I or Ellen, or any other human on this Earth? Obviously he was. Then why were we worshipping him, as if he were a god? Why were we hailing his name with such reverence and devotion? Hitler was the last person we should have been admiring. He had done nothing apart from separating our common bonds. I suddenly realized that it was he who almost led me to believe that Jews were inferior to me. It was he, who almost led me to believe that we were all more different than we were alike. But I realized then, that this is not so. We are all alike in that we are each unique. We each have our own personality, as well as heritages, cultures, and most importantly, lives. We each have a life to live, and each one of us wants to make it the best we possibly can. We each achieve this goal in different ways, but we all have this goal in common. As people, we are so alike . . .

The girl sitting next to me taps me, interrupting my thoughts. She hands me a sheet of paper. I do not hesitate, I simply pass it on.

In my conference with Sangeeta, I learned more about her background. Her father came from India to earn a Master's of Business Administration at UC–Berkeley, then went back to India to marry her mother, who studied as a Certified Public Accountant after they returned to the Bay area. Her father worked for Fireman's Fund and now is a retired consultant in business. Her mother worked at home as an accountant, but eventually stopped to spend more time with her children. Sangeeta has an older sister still at home.

Sangeeta said that she had lots of plots in her head to begin with. She felt there were many different points of view from which she could choose—any nationality, religion—everybody has a different point of view. But the first one she tried, that of a German girl growing up and coming to a realization of what was going on, is the one she stuck with. She didn't try any others.

Sangeeta didn't try the role of a Jewish boy or girl because the whole storyline would be different. Jewish teenagers were not given a choice; they were carried away by the laws. That wouldn't work, Sangeeta felt; she wanted a story about a choice, a decision. At age fifteen or sixteen she feels that people make very important choices about their opinions and their life. She tends to think carefully about decisions and gets caught up in them.

I'm sort of in the process, I suppose, of forming my opinions. I do that from a variety of sources, as Nina did, from my parents, from school, from my friends, and from reading a lot. I tend to try to look at both sides of the issue, as she did, and I guess that's really important because that is how she came to her decision.

Sangeeta clearly saw herself in her story. Decision making was important to her; the characteristics she assigns to Nina and her friend, Ellen—inquisitive, quiet and studious—are primary aspects of her own personality. Sangeeta also hoped to go to medical school.

Sangeeta talks to her parents about everything, and that seeped into her story. Although she feels that both her parents have strong opinions about issues, Sangeeta talks a lot with her mother and takes her opinion into consideration when forming her own. But she doesn't blindly follow what her mother says, nor does her mother expect her to. In general, Sangeeta thinks her mother's opinions are not as strong as those of Nina's mother in the story. But if her mother were in a similar situation, Sangeeta thinks she would react similarly. It does seem a parallel situation to Sangeeta, as she thinks about it, but she wasn't aware of it as she wrote.

Sangeeta wrote her story easily. She revised little, except the part after Nina spoke with her mother and before she made her decision. Sangeeta wanted to make Nina's thought process highly realistic; she went over and over that part trying to get it right. She wasn't completely pleased because it didn't seem smooth enough. In general, Sangeeta is seldom pleased with her writing. She is always reading books and comparing her writing to them, unconsciously, she thinks.

Sangeeta had no trouble with her ending. She wanted Nina to be decisive at the end:

I know with me at times when I really have to make a decision, right before my mind will be racing flip sides. But as soon as the time comes I will have a very strong decision I will follow, and I won't think back about it. That's another way I really brought myself in there.

Sangeeta felt support for her writing in many ways. She read an amazing number of books and wrote brief reports for ten of them for extra credit. She feels she got the idea of writing from the point of view of a student in school from one of our hand-outs in class. Two friends read her story in class and gave helpful suggestions about revising sentences. Sangeeta's sister helped by proofreading.

I noticed that Sangeeta's story did not seem to be pinned down too concretely. The girls didn't even have German names, and I could not find a specific location mentioned. I knew that Sangeeta knew as much history as anyone in the class. Why had she been so vague historically, especially since we had been specific about requesting historicity?

Sangeeta confirmed that she didn't give the city a name. She just stuck it anywhere in Germany, she said.

> It really didn't matter where it was, I don't think. It could be anywhere, or even in other countries. I made it historical because the conflict was about whether or not to join the Nazi movement. But I tried to play down the historical significance to make it more of a thing that could be applied to any time.

Sangeeta was trying to make a universal statement; how can we ever predict what students will do? But she did consider carefully some specific historical problems. She wondered whether girls went to college in early Nazi Germany. When she found a book that mentioned a girl who was a second-year medical student, that seemed acceptable. Sangeeta also thought that there probably was no Hitler Youth Group for girls, only for boys. She invented one, based on the one for boys. She says she never considered the possibility of letting her main character be a boy.

"At this age most boys think in a very different way from girls. For instance, you don't think of boys going to their mother and talking to her, or even to their father. I couldn't get a good male perspective. I couldn't have put myself in her shoes if it was a boy."

Sangeeta turned out to be the student most openly enthusiastic about our method of teaching. By the end of our conference, we were each finishing the other's sentences, we thought so much alike. Here is Sangeeta's account of how this unit affected her:

> Before this unit, and it wasn't due to lack of interest in history because I am very interested in history, especially ancient history, but before this unit I would despise going to history class. For some reason the class was boring to me, no offense to Mrs. Danielson. For some reason, I don't know why, about a couple of weeks into the unit I started looking forward to third period [history]. I like going into depth in subjects rather than just learning unsubstantial pieces. I like to learn in depth whatever I choose. In history you just get dates and facts. You don't get how people felt and how they lived. If something happened in 1925, you don't associate how it affected people. But it is lots more interesting if you can relate it to a person. It makes more sense. You can think about how you would feel in that position. I think the people part is really important, because you find out how they reacted, what they did, and you can use it in your daily life, also how you can prevent it, if it is something like the Holocaust, from happening again.

I learned as much about dates and names as I usually do. But it was a plus because you got to learn about people as well. It wasn't compromising at all. Though a lot of people won't admit it, this unit affected a lot of us profoundly. I know it did with me. I knew the events, I knew the times, but I didn't really know what had happened. . . .

The other way [names and dates] you tend just to forget it totally. If you asked me what I learned at the beginning of the year, I couldn't tell you. Memorize it for the test, and that's it. That's how it goes. But with this, if you ask me anything about the Holocaust, I'll tell you. You really soak up a lot more. . . . If you understand the feelings, then the other stuff sort of clicks in place. Once you see how people think, then it all clicks in place. Then some abstract date or place suddenly turns alive because you know where it is and what the people are like. It must be because we're people that's how we understand things.

With Sangeeta our method hit paydirt. But most of our students reacted with unusual enthusiasm to our story assignment. There were none of the usual groans and protests, and only two or three students even had trouble getting started. One girl, however, never turned in a story. Here is how Marie explained that in my conference with her.

When I first heard about the assignment, I was very excited until I started thinking about it. I wanted it to be really good, but in order for it to be really good, it would have to have happened to me. Then I could write a good story. But it didn't happen to me, and it's so disrespectful to write about something like that.

At first I wanted to have a Jewish character. Then I thought for all those people who did live through it, you have no idea. . . . I could write they were taken to this camp, they lived here, and had this kind of name. That is all specific. But as for the feelings, I could never do that. A lot of my writing is all feelings, how the person feels. I was trying to imagine what they must feel like, and I thought, "How can you do that?" I guess part of me didn't want to know either. It kind of scared me to know how they felt.

I also had a hard time imagining what it would be like when they took away so much of their freedom. I really cannot sympathize with that. I've never had that happen to me, which I'm very thankful for. I couldn't imagine what it would be like for someone to come into my house and say I can't stay there anymore.

I got the first paragraph done, and I wasn't happy with it at all. There were so many different excuses. I was in the process of writing a paper for English, and I had my mind on that. I wanted to give all my time to that. I had too much to think about. I could see myself going so far with it, and it would end up destroying itself, or being some masterpiece. You could be any nationality, sex, age. I just got confused.

My stepdad's parents are Russian, Polish in fact. How about that? I didn't think about that. I could have called up my grandmother, but I don't think she would have talked to me about that. It would have been really interesting if I could find somebody and write their story. It would be a real story. But as far as making one up and trying to imitate the feelings they felt, that seemed too fake to me.

This is the first time I've revolted against an assignment. I don't regret it, except for the grade, because I am glad that I can express my feelings on it, that somebody's here to listen to me. Because a lot of teachers would not do that. They wouldn't understand; they wouldn't care to understand. Not that it makes a great difference, but it does to me.

I hate to admit it, but Marie got lost in the shuffle for a time. We realized that she did not turn in a first draft, but she seemed to be underway on her story the day that other students read each other's first drafts. If we had managed to conference with her early in her process, we might have been able to help her think her way through to a story. There were several possibilities. Marie might have been helped to rein in her sense of audience so that it did not include real Jewish victims but only her teachers and peers. Or she might have shifted to biography, safer than fiction, and have written about a real person's experiences, perhaps her stepgrandmother's. Or, Marie might have written a piece about why she resisted this assignment.

In any case, Marie's response showed us how misleading it is for us teachers to focus solely on the product of our assignments. Here we had no product at all from the student in the class who turned out to have the highest degree of historical empathy and the most acute sense of audience, which we learned only through our conference with her about her process.

Marie realized that she had thought a great deal about the assignment and had experienced deep insights about herself and the historical situation. She greatly enjoyed the presentations of her peers, and she read three autobiographies of Jewish survivors. At the time of our conference she planned to finish her story and turn it in late, together with four more book reports for extra credit. She never did get the story in, but we agreed in conference that she certainly had met one of our main goals, that students would take responsibility for their own decisions.

In her evaluation of our unit, Marie wrote: "I learned a lot about myself, that I have a great many opinions about what I do and how I work in class and that my opinions are important."

One additional story by a girl is printed in Appendix A for further comparisons. As for the book reports, they turned out to be a clear-cut gender issue. Of the twenty-three book reports turned in for extra credit during the course of our project, every one was done by a girl. Were the boys reading? Why wouldn't they turn in a simple book report?

Of the eleven boys in class, about half of them were barely passing when we began the Holocaust unit. They were not involved enough to turn in their assignments. I was struck, as the first drafts of the stories came in, by the boys' interest in this assignment. Many of those barely passing seemed to come to life. The following story was written by one such student, Dennis:

War Journal

The prison bell has just gone off. The prisoners are just waking up for another day of hell. I am Hanz Schmit, comodant of this death camp. We had four people try to escape last night. None were successful. When they were caught, there belly's were sliced open and there skin was pulled off like a shirt. Other's have tried to escape but none have succeedded. Others have been burried alive for trying to escape. Others only get the gas chamber. But thats only when Im in a good mood.

It has been one of the coldest day's I can recall. We have had four prisoners freeze to death last night. We usually lose abought one hundred prisoners a year to the cold weather. The prisoners are so hungrey that when another prisoner dies they will eat the dead prisoners body. It does not help them very much. They usually get sick and die. If we do not put them in the gas chamber first.

Were expecting a train load of jews to come in today. They will be dead in a couple of months. The average life spand of the jew's in my camp is around two or three month's. They are usually put to death in the gas chamber. But some are put to death by our own special way's. Torture is one of our favorate things to do. It gives us all a certain kind of adrenallen rush. A certain feel of power so to say.

Hitler had made one of the greatest speaches of his life. The whole country is behind him. More and more people are blaming the jews for the problems this country is in. Thats where my job comes in. All I do is kill jews. Its something that I enjoy very much. Life would not be worth living if I could not do what I do know. This is what I was ment to be in life. This is my calling.

Today is my birthday. I have gotten gift's from all my guard's One of them made me a lamp shade made from genuine jew's skin. But they all chiped in and bought me a buatiful sweater. They are great friend's. The best a man could want. For a celebration we are going to kill about two hundred jew's. What a time I will have doing this. Killing people is my most favorite thing to do. We have many way's to kill the jew's. One of my favorite way's to kill the jew's is by letting wild dog's go on a rampage on the prisoner's.

Today is the day we get a new train load of prisoners. They will be put to death, unknowingly, in the gas chambers. We will experiment without consent unthinkable projects to further our own means as a superior race. Torture is unlimited to the end result. I will be acknowledged for my accomplishments and loyalty to the party. Scientists and Doctors are awaiting their victim's arrival. I will make a conscious effort to attend the experiments. I will gain power, acceptance and respect for my participation in the destruction of a no class society.

The morning after my 45th birthday I got a letter from my wife, Helga, and our five children, Heinz, Heidi, Kurt, Karl and little Frederick. They live in the Black Forest. Our family owns and runs a small brewery. Oh, how I miss home. I look forward to the time when this part of my life is behind me and I can be with my family again. In the meantime, the party is my life and my dedication is to the Nazi party. Heil Hitler!

Some of the lower ranking soldiers express their eagerness to perform their daily tasks. Whatever the duties include, no matter how cruel, they volunteer their services. Loyalty is the common link. The superior race is the common goal. We are undivided in our commitment. A weak link in the chain is cut and discarded. The chain is strenthened again and again. Tossing the remains to the dust. No memories, no regrets.

Only 10% of the German population are Nazi's. The party's goal is to increase this to at least 50% of the population with Hitler as our leader. There is no doubt in my mind this will become reality with the greatness he has achieved in such a short time. He was Time magazine's "man of the year" in 1942. The world has yet to see the wrath of his legacy.

People have heard rumors of the Nazi "death camps." Their reputations don't compare to their reality. Most of the German people are unaware of their existance or their purpose. The rumor's that circulate are too horid for anyone to believe

We have invaded Russia. We were devastated by the retaliation that Russia took upon Germany. It almost looks like the beginning of the end for Germany. Hitler is ordering that all death camps kill as many Jew's as possible. Hundreds of thousands to date have been exterminated. All the death camps on the outskirts of Germany are having to move their prisoner's to central locations.

Hitler is ordering his own air force bomb German cities. If he can not have complete power . . . no one will. People are fleeing the country in disbelief and total confusion. Without the strength of the party to lead them they are left helpless and hopeless.

Food supplies are gone, my health is suffering and I fear for my life. I have not heard nor do I know what has happened to my family. Even I can not believe the war will continue much longer. The Germans are being defeated every way they turn. The end is eminate.

Dennis sits in the front row by the door, usually with a red baseball cap pulled down over his face. With clear, olive skin, dark wavy hair, and a Spanish surname, I thought he might be Hispanic. In class he never said a word. I had to wait until I could engage him in some before-class conversation to hear from his speech that English is his mother tongue.

During my interview with Dennis I learned that his father, a construction worker, is Spanish and from New Mexico. His mother, who works at a bank, has parents from Germany.

Dennis's story contains some impressive use of the English language. He has trouble with spelling and punctuation, but not with conveying emotion with words. Look again at this paragraph:

Some of the lesser ranking soldiers express their eagerness to perform their daily tasks. Whatever the duties include, no matter how cruel, they volunteer their services. Loyalty is the common link. The superior race is the common goal. We are undivided in our commitment. A weak link is cut and discarded. The chain is strengthened again and again. Tossing the remains to the dust. No memories, no regrets.

In my conference with Dennis I opened by commending him on this excellent paragraph, since I couldn't be particularly enthusiastic about the pro-Nazi perspective of the story's content. I learned that he had written every word of his story. He felt he really got into the writing, that it represented the viewpoint of his grandfather, who died about five years ago. His grandfather had been a regular soldier in the German army during World War II and had come over to the United States right after the war. Dennis had lived near him, saw him frequently, and loved him. "He was a big guy who was really nice to me," Dennis commented.

His grandfather told Dennis about Germany, about how superior the Germans were, and about how he wished there would be another uprising of Germans. Sometimes his grandfather would tell Dennis not to talk to Jews.

Dennis says that his mom still shares some of her father's attitudes, since she was raised on them. Dennis's own attitudes have changed; he doesn't think there will ever be another German uprising, or that one race is better than everybody else. He doesn't think it would be acceptable for Germany to start killing Jews, but he does think that "having one leader in Germany would be all right, if he was right about what he was doing."

Dennis felt clear that he was telling his story from his grandfather's point of view, and because he was, he had problems with the ending. Here's how he analyzed it:

> I got stuck at the end, when I was trying to think of some way to end it. I kept thinking about how they [Germans] tried to invade Russia and got wasted. I tried to remember our classroom discussion. I had some notes written down . . . I was writing the main story kind of out of my grandfather's viewpoint, or writing *about* my grandfather. He would have probably wanted more about German superiority, probably wouldn't have liked my ending, probably would want me to just leave it at that. That's why I got stuck. I was thinking about that a lot. Should I leave it [Germany] as being great or should I write about the whole fall? I decided this was better because it tells what happened at the end of the war.

Dennis worked hard on his story. We noticed that his final draft differed almost entirely from his first draft, which was filled with descriptions of cruelty, castration of "fags," and hate. When we asked why he had changed it, he replied: "I thought this would be better. I didn't use much of my first draft at all. It was easier not to look at it."

Perhaps Dennis omitted his first draft in part because he thought we might not like it. But he seemed secure that he was making his own decision, and he presented his process as a dialogue between himself and his grandfather, perhaps mediated by his mother.

A friend in another class also helped, as Dennis told us when we asked him, "But why a death camp commandant?"

> I thought he was interesting to write about because everybody [in class] was going to write about a Jew, and nobody wanted to write about what it would be like on the other side. It was the first thing I thought about. I talked about it with a friend in another class. He was doing the same type of story. We talked about what happened back then and what we could use in the stories, in case one didn't have the information.

When we asked Dennis how he made his story historical, he responded that his whole story was historical "because it's all the truth. It's what happened back then, and how nobody knew about it. Everybody heard rumors, but they didn't know about it until the end of the war." When we asked if he included anything whose historical accuracy he questioned, he mentioned the lamp made out of Jewish skin. He was told about that in class, but he wondered about it. "It feels kind of sick. Who'd want to skin somebody?"

This student, who previously had done as little as possible in this class, had clearly carried on a thoughtful imaginary dialogue with his dead grandfather, conferred with his mother and a friend about his dilemmas, written pages of excellent prose, and put his heart into history. The first part of the process was, for him, to write pages that many teachers might consider disgusting and inappropriate. But Linda and I accepted his offering as I believe that teachers must do to encourage writing.

When Linda and I allowed Dennis to write what he really cared about, this let him connect with his grandfather, his understanding of Hitler, and the Holocaust. We didn't know until after we graded Dennis's story, when I was able to conference with him for half an hour, that he was writing from his grandfather's point of view. We thought it was his own. But since we refrained from criticism, Dennis was able—through his writing—to discover that his own attitudes had changed; they were no longer what his grandfather's were.

When Dennis evaluated his experience with this unit, he said

> What was good? I got to learn alot about the Nazis. And I'm German, so I got to learn what I'm about.
> What was not so good? Learning that the Nazis got wiped out. It was kind of sad.
> How valuable was the writing? It was worthless. [Maybe he thought this referred to the journal writing, instead of to the story?]
> How did this unit affect your attitude toward history? It made me happy to be German.
> What did you learn about yourself? To be proud about what I am.

Dennis was one of five boys who chose to be a Nazi. The other six boys selected three Jewish roles, two non-Nazi Germans, and one Allied prisoner of war.

The boy's story that follows explores being Jewish during the Holocaust. The story belongs to Rob, a little guy who hides out under a baseball cap, never says a word in class, and is one of those students you might not notice for days at a time. Rob had a C+ average before this unit.

I was not very old in 1938, just eleven, and a little thing. All that anyone could talk about was Hitler. He must be an important guy in Germany. I would ask my father a lot of questions about this guy they call Hitler, like why didn't he like German Jews? I got the same answer from him all the time "because he didn't." How could I ever find out anything if he never answered any of my questions? I only knew what the radio said. The radio said that something had happened. A Jewish boy had killed a German man. That night the Germans ran through the streets and killed and rounded up a lot of Jews. That night had a special name: Kristallnacht. I asked my father what Kristallnacht meant but all he said was "Ssht. I'm listening." Ever since Hitler started so much trouble, my father didn't have anytime to play or even to talk to me. My mother was the same way, she wouldn't answer any of my questions.

On the night of June 14, 1940, some German soldiers raided every house on our street except ours. I guess we were just lucky that there was no more room left in the trucks. By this time, I was not allowed outside of my house. My parents said that if I were to go outside of my house then I would get picked up just like our friends. I didn't have any clothes except the clothes on my back. We must have hidden in our house for at least six months, living on just bread and hardly any meat. We probably had meat once a month. I was to the point of starvation, until I found some meat just laying in the middle of the street. My mother's words ran through my mind about a million times, "do not go outside of the house or you will get picked up just like your friends." I peered outside my door. Not seeing anyone, I raced toward the meat. All of a sudden a bunch of German soldiers surrounded me, there was nowhere to run. My mom and dad came running out to see what had happened. The German soldiers took my parents and me and put us in separate trucks. They took us to the same camp. My parents were trying to struggle to get to me, but to no avail. The German soldiers hit them over the head and knocked them out. Since my parents were so old they were put in a separate part of the camp than I was. The last time that I saw my parents was the time I saw them get hit over the head.

I heard stories of what had happened to them. It took me a long time to face the fact that I was never going to see my parents again. After they had no use for me at the unknown camp they sent me to Auschwitz.

At the time that I was sent to Auschwitz I was about thirteen years old, weighing only about ninety pounds. At the present camp they fed me once a day where as at the other camp I was lucky if I was fed at all. It was said that they needed more healthy people at the labor camps. I was one of the twenty people randomly selected to go to the labor camps.

I was sent to the labor camp called Belzec. It was not too far from Auschwitz. It only took five days to get there. There were a lot of rules that you had to follow, or you were sent back to the death camp. You had to get up at sunrise, no breaks until the soldier says so, be at the place where food is given out on time or you will not get any, do whatever the soldiers say. If you abide by those four rules you would not get in that much trouble. Sometimes the soldiers would start beating on you and if you tried to fight back then you would be shot on sight. I have seen at least thirty people get shot in a weeks time. That is why there is a shortage of people in the labor camps. The soldiers keep on killing them. You think that you aren't going to get killed because you were moved out of the death camp, then all of a sudden you get beat to death by a couple of soldiers.

I never got in any trouble with any of the soldiers. Actually I was friends with one of them. He told me when someone was going to get beat up and he also got me some extra food. One day we were caught talking and the man in charge of the camp ordered the death of my friend. He made me pull the trigger. It was horrible, I tried to get out of it but they said that if I didn't kill him then I would be killed.

After that incident, I was set back to Auschwitz. I had to get back onto the crowded train. There was at least eighty people per train car. People were sleeping on top of each other, on top of other people's belongings, and everything. It was one of the most horrible sights that I have ever seen. The trip was miserable. There were people vomiting and there were some people that were going to the bathroom in the car. We had to put up with the smell for at least three days.

When we arrived at Auschwitz, we were loaded off of the train one by one in a straight and orderly fashion. The people that did not cooperate were killed immediately. Everyone that was on the train together was put in the same barricks. I made some friends with the other people in the same barricks. There was one particular person that I liked a lot. His name was John Atkinson Burnheim, he was a Jew also, of course. Him and I looked alike at the time. We both had black hair, brown eyes, short hair, and not that heavy. Him and I had ideas to escape, but the others did not want to take the risk of getting captured and put to death. I could see why they did not want to try to escape, but I would rather die trying to escape than be put to death slowly and painfully. There was no way that I was going to sit around and do nothing. John and I got to know one of the guards of our cell, he was really nice. I asked him why he joined the army with Hitler and he said that he had no choice. Hitler would of killed his whole family if he did not follow his command. If he was caught trying to save some of the Jews then he and his whole family would die.

A couple of years passed, which seemed like centuries, and we started to make some plans to escape from the prison camp. We stayed up for a very long time every night to make the plans. We picked out the weakest parts of the camp with the help of our German soldier friend. He made sure that we stayed healthy and well fed. If it was not for him then we would of probably have starved to death. I probably would not be alive to tell this story to you.

It took us a long time to get up the courage to try to escape. At the last second when we were about to try our daring escape, John was woke up by a German soldier and taken away. I could hear him screaming all the way down the hall. I started to cry, he was the only person that was left that I could talk to. After he was taken away, all of our hard work was wasted. It took me a long time to forget about him. I never really did forget about him but I decided that it was either him or me.

There was no one that was left that would try and escape from the camp with me. I begged and begged for someone to at least help me try and escape. A new guy came in and I knew that he was the one that was going to try and escape with me. I could see him scoping the place out with his eyes. He looked out over the guard tower, "don't even think about trying to get passed them," I said. "Behind them are four rows of barbed wire fence."

"I'm just looking," he said.

When we were put back in our cells, we got to know each other pretty well. His name is John Adam Keefe. He was a German who was caught helping a Jewish family hide from the German soldiers. His family was killed on the spot. The only reason that they needed him was for his work.

A week has passed and we have come up with a good plan of escaping. At the last second John is having second thoughts. He said that we should wait another week before we try and escape. It felt a little weird but I said all right. The next few days I didn't see John that much. I didn't think much of it. He said that they had him cleaning out some of the offices for the higher authorities.

The day has come and we were all ready to gather all of our materials needed to escape when a bunch of German soldiers jumped on me and took me to a cell all by myself. I could hear the German soldier that was in charge say "good job John."

I was yelling and screaming all the way to my new cell. I couldn't understand why he would do such a horrible thing. I trusted the guy and he blaintingly defied that trust. What could of made him do something like that? I would never have that question answered. I think I knew the answer. He was probably a German that was posing as a prisoner so they could find out who was trying to escape and how.

I got word that I was to be killed the next day. That is when I started to write this story. I wanted the people in the future to know what the Germans were like and how they treated the Jews. I found a good hiding place for the story. It must have been good if you just found it. The next day has rolled along. It looked like a good day to die.

"Just kidding, there is never a good day to die." I can hear the soldiers coming down the hall to get me. They drug me blindfolded to a big brick wall. They took the blindfold off so that I could witness my own death. The leader said, because it was in German I'm not really sure what he said but this is what I think he said, "ready, aim, fire!!!" The only bullet that I felt was the first. "AAAHHH!!!!"

Rob told us in his interview that he chose to be this little Jewish kid, Jason, because "there would be a lot of information that I could personally put myself in the place of the kid. I know how it feels. I'm a kid. I know how a kid thinks. I thought it'd make a pretty good story, so that's why I select it. There'd be a lot to write about, I thought."

But where did he get his idea, we pressed. "I think the Jewish kids were hit the hardest. Even though the parents were killed, it was really hard for them to keep going. They didn't have anything to live for. They had no one to support them. They had no one to turn to if they had problems. I think they were the hardest hit."

But why a Jewish kid, we persisted. "Around the class a lot of people were writing about German soldiers and German kids, and I just thought I might be a little different and write about a Jewish kid instead. There's other people who wrote about Jewish families together. But I chose to write about this 'cause I didn't hear about people writing about a Jewish kid getting separated from his family."

Rob told us he didn't think he could write about a Nazi kid. "I couldn't put myself in their spot. I could not just watch people getting killed. I couldn't have my father come home and say, 'Oh, yeah, I killed so and so today. It was fun.' I couldn't write about that.

It would be too emotional. This is emotional, yeah, but I mean I don't like it about racial stuff, and I wouldn't be able to write about it because of that. If I was writing, I would say that I was ashamed of my father."

Rob had lived in Mississippi with his mom and dad, both white, until he was seven years old. When his parents divorced, Rob went back to Mississippi twice, once when he was in the eighth grade. He stayed for six months. Now he lives with his mom and stepdad, who have strong antiracist views. He has a brother, who is eighteen years old and feels the same way Rob does about racial issues. His grandparents, too, believed in racial equality and had black friends.

> I didn't look at black kids at the point that they're black. I looked at 'em as a person, how they acted, what they did, if they had the same interests as me. I don't look at people on the outside . . . Some of my white friends [in Mississippi] didn't like blacks, so I was sorta in the middle. I just had to let them go, cause I'm not gonna pick and choose just because they're black, because they're Jewish or whatever race they are. . . . It was more or less half and half of the white kids who would have black friends. I didn't feel isolated. If they didn't like me for who I am, then forget 'em. I'm not going to change to please someone.

When we asked Rob if he was in his story, he first thought not, but then astonished us with this connection:

> Probably when the kid looked outside the door, I looked outside. It's just like—I'm supposed to be racial [racist], but then I look outside and the big meat represents a black kid. Then I go out because I want to meet him and see what he's like. But then a bunch of white kids surround me and the black kid.

Telling stories reveals inner truths, as Rob discovers here. But in general he felt that he didn't put his own life in this story; he just thought of something original. He admitted that the outgoing people in his story represented his older brother, and that Jason, as a person, was sort of withdrawn. He didn't connect that with himself.

Rob felt that his story "flowed really good. I just sat down at the computer and started writing. It just started flowing into my head. Once I got my main ideas down, I made them descriptive. I knew what I wanted to put down and where."

The only place Rob got stuck was the beginning. He considers starting a story the hardest part, and he devoted much effort to getting started on this one. He went to a friend's house and asked the friend's stepdad, who knows a lot about Hitler, for suggestions. Both Rob and his friend's stepdad wrote down five or six possible opening sentences. The stepdad came up with, "Just eleven and a little thing," while Rob came up with "I was not very old." He liked this lead "because it starts out the story, he asks questions to his dad, he's sort of antsy, he wants to know things, and his parents won't tell him." It took Rob two days to find a lead he felt good about.

Rob felt that even on the first draft his story flowed out well. But while making revisions, he felt the story was "sort of dull." He wanted to liven it up. Linda's suggestion to him on the first draft was: "Great job. Maybe include some dialogue to liven up the story."

Rob decided that his story would be more exciting if his character, Jason, died instead of surviving. Rob also added the plans to escape and Jason's having to kill his friend, the German soldier.

"I sort of built the story on what I like to read," said Rob. "I can't write something I don't like to write. Teachers give us something to write on, and if I really like it, I can go on and on and on. But if I don't like it, I can only write maybe a paragraph. One of my friends read it. . . . Most of the kids that are going to read it are going to be my age. He thought it would be a lot better if there was a little more action. So I went back through and took out some stuff and put stuff in."

Rob felt that the readings we did in class and the photos we displayed helped him a lot. He used information from the document that we gave out about *Kristallnacht* to open his story. Reading stories written by other boys in class helped show him what he didn't want to do. They had "bunkers in them, bunkers, bunkers, bunkers. A lot of people thought the same in class. I wanted to be different and go off on my own."

Rob wondered about what the camps really looked like and what they really did to the Jews, especially in the labor camps. What kind of work did they do? How long did they work? How much did they get fed? He had to put in some information that he wasn't sure of, and he assured us that if he rewrote his story he would do more research.

Again, here is a student who put remarkable thought and integrity into his story. He connected with his past, his parents and grandparents, especially in his strong commitment to racial equality. His story, like other boys' stories, is filled with action, violence, and death. But unlike many other stories by boys, Rob chose to explore something he knows firsthand, being young. (Two other boys chose to be teenagers in their stories; the other nine chose to be adult men.) Rob's story also shows his deep concern for children. Besides Rob, only one girl chose to be an orphaned, Jewish teenager caring for young siblings. Since Rob's stepfather is in the Navy, he is away from home about half the year, leaving Rob to help his mother care for the family, which includes stepsisters who are four and six.

Rob reveals himself in his story as a quiet, reserved young man built on the solid integrity of knowing who he is. He evaluated his experience in the unit as positive.

> The unit on the holocaust enlightened me on the subject. We spent a little too much time on it, and a lot of the handouts were the same. I liked not using the [text]book; my bookbag was a lot lighter. The writing was very valuable. It showed that we understood everything that we were talking about in class. [This unit] made me want to learn more about history. [I learned] if I really tried that I could write a good story.

The boys' stories do seem to contrast with those of the girls. The boys wrote more detailed descriptions of violence. They imagined combat more often. They fantasized adulthood more often than the girls did. The count reveals that eight boys chose to be adults in their stories, while three chose to be teenagers. This contrasts with the girls, five of whom chose to be adults, while nine chose to be teenagers. The boys certainly insisted on more action than the girls.

But perhaps this only seems so on the surface, with the more aggressive boys. Let's look closely at the character that each boy created.

- Chris: A Nazi, Hitler's first general, who resigned over what he saw; wished he had killed Hitler; lots of violence described in detail.

- Erik: A Nazi lieutenant, gassed by a superior officer for spurning his sexual advance; some violence described.

- Bob: An antisocial German killed in camp; cares only for wife and children.

- Michael: A Nazi in charge of a concentration camp; caught for not wanting to fight in the frontlines; lots of violence described.

- Randy: A U.S. prisoner of war captured by Nazis, rescued by Patton's 3rd infantry; mostly violence.

- Tyler: A seventeen-year-old German who disagrees with Nazi father; commits suicide; no violence.

- Hank: An Italian businessman married to a Jew; his family is shot and he is waiting to take his life; no violence.

- Sam: A twelve-year-old Jewish boy killed with family in camp.

- Rob: A Jewish teenager who loses parents and is killed after many incidents; violence but not detailed.

- Dennis: A Nazi commandant who never repents but acknowledges Nazi loss; focuses on Nazi ideas rather than details of violence, except in first draft.
- Hosh: A fervent anti-Nazi who becomes Hitler's bodyguard and plans to kill him; much detail of cruelty and violence.

Of eleven boys, five described acts of cruelty and violence. None of the girls did. But any generalization is likely not to fit an individual story. Some boys were as nurturing and caring about family relationships as any girls, and one girl got full satisfaction from dying in combat to protect her people. Every story reflects a complex, unique, and differentiated individual personality already clearly forming at age fifteen and quickly coming into consciousness of itself.

In my conferences with students, almost every one reported that they wanted their story to be different from the others in their class. They wanted to work from other perspectives; they wanted to resist peer pressure by defining their own point of view. This phenomenon does not show up regularly in accounts of younger children's writing historical fiction (Jorgensen 1993). This confirms my hypothesis that history comes most alive for teenagers when it connects them with an awareness of their own identities.

Six

Components of History Workshop

With our combined years of experience, Linda and I were able to juggle many different elements of instruction and combine them into the complex process we called history workshop. In this chapter I want to analyze in some detail seven disparate components that we melded into history workshop.

One: Conception of History

How one views history may not seem to be an element of instruction, yet it proved to be the source from which all our other strategies flowed. If I believed that historian-robots with no point of view sat down before definitive piles of documents and extracted the real facts, which they assembled into textbooks, I might be content to go through the textbook with students.

But I have never believed that. Even in my first year of teaching I frequently muttered, "Well, the textbook must be mistaken about that," to the horror of my European-American students. I can't remember my African-American students ever being disturbed.

There is no definitive pile of documents for historians to examine. There are no historian-robots without points of view. The facts can be listed, but the moment a narrative is composed, a paragraph shaped, someone is interpreting the facts.

Thirty years ago secondary students may not have realized this, but today they do. They hear about the multiple interpretations of Columbus on TV and in the newspaper. They know that not even the maps in their texts are accurate since the Soviet Union unraveled. They come from communities and cultures that tell different stories about history than the textbooks do. If students believe that teachers don't understand that history is a set of competing narratives, they can resist and argue with their instructors or, more likely—given the balance of power—tune out as completely as possible.

History workshop is an approach to teaching that attempts to demonstrate how historians understand their work. Since World War II the history profession has greatly expanded to include women and people of color. Tape recorders have put into historical record the voices of people who would not have left written records. People working at history have transformed what it is. No longer limited to constitutional and political topics focused on government leaders and wars, history now encompasses social and family history, changes in sexual behavior, immigration, sports, prison, food, ecology, media, whatever. Every aspect of culture is addressed and included by historians; content that used to be considered economics or anthropology or sociology becomes history when those topics are looked at as they develop over time. As historian Tom Holt says, "In history something is always developing, breaking down, emerging, transforming, growing, or declining. Otherwise, it's sociology." (1990, p.11)

Objectivity in history was long a dream of the historical profession, as Peter Novick discusses it in *That Noble Dream: The "Objectivity Question" and the American Historical Profession (1988)*. With the scientific revolution eventually came scientific history—the attempt to study evidence using rigorous methodology, eliminate personal bias, and record history as it really occurred, "*wie es eigentlich gewesen,*" in the well-known words of German historian Leopold van Ranke. In Novick's view the American historical profession has gone through four periods: first, enthroning objectivity; besieging it; then reconstructing it; and finally, abandoning objectivity and accepting a multiplicity of interpretations. The current crisis in objectivity extends beyond the historical profession, of course; it is part of the contemporary intellectual climate that sees all knowledge as constructed by people in a specific context. To teach effectively teachers must also seek to understand these issues about the nature of history.

Two: Primary Sources

As discussed in chapter 1, primary sources are those created by eyewitnesses or participants. Primary sources are distinguished from secondary sources, which were created after the event. Primary sources are also called firsthand sources, especially in elementary school. By high school, the primary source most often used is a written document, although we assist our students significantly if we use the whole range of primary sources: artifacts, visual images (photos, maps, drawings), recordings, and living people, in addition to written documents.

In our unit Linda and I used mostly visual images and written documents. For our in-class readings, variety and human interest were the two basic criteria by which we selected our primary documents. We wanted to avoid boring, difficult-to-read, legal or official documents that would most likely repel rather than attract students. We wanted to have some documents on which students could practice their analytical skills, and other more personal accounts that would appeal to students' emotions and show them what everyday life was like for a variety of people.

With the wealth of material available about the Holocaust, our chief task was to narrow our selection of documents. We made the selection of readings using three criteria: topics we identified as essential, a variety of both narrative and expository readings, and a variety of perspectives. In addition to readings, we added other kinds of primary sources: a guest speaker, photos, two videos, and maps. The final list of primary sources that we used is shown in Figure 6–1.

All of these readings are brief. Most are two pages long and the longest is four pages. We photocopied class sets of documents, used them only in class, and collected them for the next class. Reading the documents in class took lots of time, but it ensured that everyone read the basic material, and it left homework time for extra reading, talking to friends and family, and writing.

When reading a primary document, our students answered the basic questions: Who wrote it? (What kind of person? What point of view?) When? Where? What does it tell us? This approach was new to the students and we did not have enough copies to send documents home, where there might have been more time for reflection.

But in the future, as students become more accustomed to encountering primary documents, we could deepen the level of questioning. We could ask: how and why was this document produced, and how does that affect its trustworthiness? What is it silent about? What does it leave out? What does it assume? For whom was it written?

On reflection, we think our beginning work with primary sources worked extremely well. Students, on the whole, much preferred them to the textbook. They liked the variety of the sources

Figure 6–1
List of Primary Sources

Topic	Title	Type	Perspective	Source
Racist ideas	A. memory of third grader, Nazi doctrine	Nar.	Nazi	FH&O, p. 19
	B. excerpt from Robert Bennett Bean, The Races of Man (1932)	Exp.	Racist	
Nazi Documents	A. First Program of Nazi Party, 1920	Exp.	Nazi	another teacher
	B. Mein Kampf (selections), 1923	Exp.	Nazi	same
	C. Nuremberg Laws, 1935	Exp.	Nazi	another teacher
Kristallnacht	A. a German Catholic remembers	Nar.	non-Nazi	FH&O
	B. article on 50th observation	Exp.	Balanced	New York Times (10.29.88)
	C. account in college text	Exp.	Balanced	Brinton, Christopher & Wolff, A History of Civilization, 2nd ed. II, 1960
Resistance	A. Choiceless Choice	Exp.	Jewish	FH&O
	B. Decision to resist	Exp.	Jewish	FH&O
Concentration Camps	Hoess, "Taking Lives at Auschwitz"	Nar.	Nazi	FH&O
Who Helped?	A. Rescue in Denmark	Nar.	Rescue	FH&O
	B. People who helped	Nar.	Rescue	FH&O
Homosexuals	"Pink Triangles"	both	Homosexual	draft FH&O
Camps: Psychology	Viktor Frankl, "Delusion of Reprieve"	Nar.	Jewish	FH&O
Camps: Liberation	Clara Green, "The Last Day"	Nar.	Jewish	Michael Selzer, Deliverance Day: The Last Hours at Dachau (1978)
Maps	"The Jews of Europe, 1937–41"		Jewish	Martin Gilbert, Jewish History Atlas, rev. ed., (1969)
Photos	"The Nazi Holocaust," series II		Balanced	Documentary Photo Aids, n.d., Box 956, Mt. Dora, FL 32757
Guest	German who was a teenager during the war			School secretary
Videos	"Hitler: Portrait of Tyranny"		anti-Nazi	another teacher
	"The Wave"			

(readings, photos, videos, speaker), and they liked the variety in perspective. A few students commented that the primary sources were too much alike. They seemed to mean too Jewish, too anti-Nazi, in perspective. They thought that having more from a German perspective, both Nazi and non-Nazi, would make it all more understandable. They wanted to comprehend how it could all have happened. We think we balanced the selections reasonably well, although the next time we would probably add a selection or two from a book we just located edited by Ernest Klee, Willi Dressen, and Volker Riess, "The Good Old Days": The Holocaust As Seen By Its Perpetrators and Bystanders (1988).

The literature on the Holocaust is so rich that I must mention a few other titles. Another general sourcebook is Roselle Chartock and Jack Spencer, eds., The Holocaust Years: Society on Trial (1978). Two historical fictions about the Danish resistance are Lois Lowry's, Number the Stars (1990), and Carol Matas's, Lisa's War (1991). A good source of primary documents are Milton Meltzer's two books, Never to Forget: The Jews of the Holocaust (1977) and Rescue: The Story of How Gentiles Saved Jews in the Holocaust (1991). Another amazing primary source is Yitzhak Zuckerman, Surplus of Memory: Chronicle of the Warsaw Ghetto Uprising (1993). Two general histories include Nightmare in History (1992) by Miriam Chaikin, and Barbara Rogasky's, Smoke and Ashes (1988). An unforgettable story that works well with our workshop is Fred Uhlman's, Reunion (1986), about two schoolboys, one the son of a Jewish surgeon, the other the son of aristocratic Christian Germans. The young men enjoy an idyllic friendship in 1932 as the clouds roll over their doomed world.

Some teachers consider the selection of suitable primary sources an obstacle to implementing history workshop. They hesitate to increase their workload by adding research assignments. Many are uncertain about where to locate primary sources.

Most teachers, however, can ask the school or city librarian for help or consult the school or local library catalog. College teachers and librarians are another source, as are local and state history societies. Book stores can be a major help. Consult the subject catalog of Books in Print and order a few titles, or browse in used bookstores. Assign students to locate primary sources; why should teachers do all the work? Don't forget family collections. Professional history organizations publish collections of primary sources for secondary teachers; I have listed some of these in Appendix B. It only takes one document or one story to start.

Three: Multiple Perspectives

The third essential feature of history workshop is its variety of perspectives, or points of view. When I tell my Jewish friends that I
taught a unit on the Holocaust in which I encouraged my students to
create any character they want in Hitler's Europe—even Nazi characters—many of them say, "Why would you want to do that?"

When the teacher next door to us heard about our unit, she
couldn't wait to try it. We described to her the essential components,
and she carried them out at once, planning for two weeks instead of
six. As primary documents she used almost exclusively rescue stories, and all her students created characters who rescued. They created no Nazi characters.

In our class we encouraged students to create any character from
all the possibilities. When we first discussed this, several boys considered being Hitler. As described in chapter 4, Linda resisted this
possibility. Might this not develop their neo-Nazi tendencies? Why
would we encourage them to identify with people who committed
terrible wrongs? Taking their cue from Linda's initial response, no
one dared to be Hitler, even though Linda explained the next day that
it would be fine with her. Instead, they chose to be bodyguards or
assistants, not Hitler himself.

I believe that most people have a capacity to act with cruelty
against others in self-interest. This is an aspect of human nature that
is not helpful to deny, since we are better prepared to control our
cruelty if we acknowledge and examine it. Some people can be cruel
in fairly benign situations; often only extreme circumstances can
provoke others to express cruelty. A few people, perhaps, cannot be
driven to cruelty for any reason.

When students create a story character who is a death camp commandant, they understand that under similar circumstances they
might become such a person. In their stories, students deal imaginatively with the consequences of such behavior, and they hear the
reactions of their classmates. They have a chance to examine what it
might be like to behave in such a way.

To examine further the question, "Does this assignment encourage neo-Nazi tendencies among students?" I want to discuss briefly
each of the stories written by the six students who chose to be Nazis.
In chapter 5, Dennis' story showed how he wrote from his grandfather's Nazi perspective and how, through his writing, Dennis realized that he did not agree with his grandfather.

Four other boys chose Nazi roles. Hosh and Erik wrote stories
included in Appendix A. Hosh's character pretended to be a Nazi to
get close enough to Hitler to kill him. Erik created a Nazi lieutenant

to show that you were not safe even if you became a Nazi. In a story not included in this text, Mike created a death camp commandant who enjoyed his work but who, when transferred to combat duty, resisted, hid, and was killed by the Nazis. In his conference, Mike said, "I wanted to be a Jew, but I didn't know enough. I created a character who the Nazi party wanted, and he was too scared to get out of it. I gave him a bad background [reform school] to make him a Nazi. I got stuck at the end because I didn't know how to make him turn good."

The fifth boy's story written with a Nazi main character was by Chris, who portrayed a Nazi general who resigned because of his experiences and who wished that he had killed Hitler himself.

The only girl who chose a Nazi role, Liz, did so deliberately to see if she could imagine herself in an abhorrent situation; she wanted to try to understand the people involved. Her character, married to a Nazi soldier who dies in the war, discovers that her mother was Jewish and flees to Switzerland, repudiating Nazism. Liz commented:

> I wanted to put myself in the place of someone else so I could really understand where they're coming from, not just sit back and be really arrogant and say, "Look at these terrible people, what they're doing." I wanted to explore the other side of the story. I wonder what it really was like to be a Nazi, and to think you're on the top of the world . . . There's so many hate groups out there, so many people who think they're on top of the world, who think that everybody else who is not white, or not black, is just scum of the earth. But I also believe there are a lot of good people in the world who really want to help and who really care about people's feelings. I don't know if it could happen again, but it could.

I believe these comments show that teenagers, perhaps more flexible in their empathies than adults, can explore the thinking of people whose actions they condemn. They realize that condemnation does not lead to understanding, which they seek. If we had not given our students permission to explore the roles of Nazi sympathizers, I believe we would have placed a serious limitation on the scope of their comprehension and on their willingness to become involved in this assignment.

In our class no one was willing to defend a contemporary neo-Nazi position. But some classrooms contain such students, and we needed to be ready to deal with that possibility. What would we have done if some of our students had defended killing Jews, homosexuals, or African Americans?

Instead of rushing in with a rebuttal, either our own or one from another student, the position should be examined like any other. I might ask other students questions like, "What beliefs might some-one have to take this position? What assumptions lie under this opinion? From what background could your classmate be coming?" The student with neo-Nazi opinions could explain and defend him- or herself; other students could probe and challenge. Only in this way can the class examine the full range of possible opinions, and students with beliefs that reject tolerance of diversity can experience enough respect to begin to question their positions.

Multiple perspectives on history exist both in the outside world and inside our classrooms. Heterogenous classes of students with diverse skills, cultures, and backgrounds, as characterized our class at Novato High, work best because they reflect the complexity of the world. If teachers cannot accept the multiplicity of interpretations outside our classrooms, that reality is mirrored in our attitudes within our classrooms. Then we reward students who share our perspectives, and we condemn or ignore others whose interpreta-tions we find unsettling. We give some students status over others, often unwittingly. When teachers bring materials with multiple per-spectives into our classrooms, we validate more of our students and will be rewarded with their engagement in their studies.

Four: Journal Writing

"Quick-writes"—writing in journals for ten minutes at the beginning of class—were an established routine in Linda's class. She assigned a topic, anything she thought might spark a reaction, and students were expected to sit down, get organized, and write nonstop. During these ten minutes, Linda took roll and got her business done.

We continued this procedure during history workshop, modify-ing it to connect the topics to the lessons. Since we had so little time for our material, we used the journal writing as an integral part of our lesson. Occasionally we assigned a journal writing as homework. Once in a while we gave out a primary document both to read and to respond to during journal-writing time. And, of course, sometimes we omitted journal writing altogether when other activities filled the period.

The seventeen topics we used for journal writing during our unit's twenty-six lessons included the following:

1. Write about what you know and/or associate with Nazism. What would you like to find out about it?

2. Fill in the sheet on stereotypes.

3. What is the definition of race as it pertains to humans? What have you been taught? Does it differ from what you experience or see with your own eyes?

4. Write your reaction to today's readings, Mein Kampf and the Nuremberg Laws (completed as homework the night before).

5. Why do you think people supported Hitler as their ruler? How did he maintain his power over the people?

6. What decisions have you made about the character you're going to write about? Describe what actual events she or he will experience.

7. How might Jews and non-Jews have resisted the Nazis? Or did they? Why might they have complied?

8. Read Choiceless Choice and write a response to what you read.

9. Write your thoughts about "Taking Lives at Auschwitz."

10. What facts have you learned so far about Nazism and the Holocaust? What more do you want to find out?

11. Read the Victor Frankl selection and write about your response to it.

12. Briefly describe your progress on your story. What's it about? What's hard about writing it? What's easy? What's good?

13. Write your thoughts on the subject of homosexuality.

14. In your opinion should the United States have used the atom bomb on Hiroshima and Nagasaki? Why or why not?

15. What are the lessons we should learn from studying the Holocaust?

16. Read "The Last Day" and respond to it.

17. What do you think should have been done with the Nazis who were personally responsible for the death and torture of so many people?

We created these topics to fit into our lessons as they evolved. Students enjoyed this writing. It certainly seemed to contribute to their self-confidence, their fluency in writing, and the delineation of their ideas. It opened class with the satisfying feeling that everyone was being productive. I regret only that we did not immediately collect the journals, for they contained valuable feedback that we could have used, giving us clues about where to go with the next lessons and how to help individual students.

Five: History Talk Groups

We had more difficulty with History Talk Groups than with any other feature of history workshop. There were many reasons: students were not accustomed to group work; initially we made the groups too large (six); we kept changing the groups instead of keeping them stable; we were not clear enough in our instructions about what students should be discussing; we were always running out of time.

The purpose of the talk groups was to give students opportunity to talk; freedom to inquire and hypothesize; and a chance to participate more informally than they can in whole-class discussion. We also wanted them to practice looking at a document critically, asking: "What is this? What is the point of view? What could this person's motive be for saying this?"

Linda and I used the basic principles of effective group work. We identified roles and asked each group to select them: facilitator, recorder, reporter. We always had the groups report out to the whole class, except when time ran out. Sometimes we had students debrief the process, asking them to analyze the difficulties they were having. Sometimes, to increase accountability, we collected the recorder's report, after insisting that every group member's opinion be described in writing.

The greatest concern for Linda and me was the selection of group members; should students choose their own groups or should we? If we allowed the students to choose, then groups based on friendship had many topics to discuss other than the Holocaust. If *we* selected the groups, the nonfriends would clam up and feel uncomfortable revealing their feelings and opinions to each other. We discussed these dilemmas with our students and found they had the same mixed responses that we did.

After experimenting with a variety of group arrangements, Linda and I concluded that four is the optimum size for a discussion group. Larger ones leave people out, and the facilitator often cannot manage to keep everyone on task. We also reached a compromise on composition—students each chose one friend as a partner, then we assigned partners to form foursomes. This arrangement seems to combine the advantages of both student-selection and teacher-selection.

Linda and I also tried several approaches to instruction. When we distributed primary sources, we sometimes listed questions for discussion right on the document. Sometimes we gave verbal instructions and posed open-ended questions like what surprised you? what did you find interesting? what are your responses?

During the unit we made a classroom poster of general questions and discussion points required for all documents. We wanted students to internalize this strategy of questioning, and we knew it would take much practice. The poster included the following:

How to Evaluate a Primary Source

1. What is the name or title of the document?
2. When was it written?
3. Who wrote the document?
4. What do you know about the writer? What would you like to know about him or her?
5. What perspective or bias is shown in the writing?
6. How does the material fit into the history of the time period?
7. Summarize what it says.
8. What does it mean? What is its purpose?
9. What don't you understand? What is confusing to you?
10. Ask questions about the document.

Students told us it was difficult to discuss firsthand accounts by Jewish victims—difficult to get past, "My, how awful!" All the material Linda and I asked students to discuss was charged with emotion and controversy. They found it difficult to reveal their feelings and opinions about the subject matter.

But the History Talk Groups provided a small, intimate group where students could explore their ideas and feelings. Students usually chose same-sex partners and preferred our assigning another same-sex pair. The following dialogue reveals a conversation among four girls who discuss a reading that provides a brief biography of eight people who rescued Jews.

Polly: I just think that . . . What was the one?

Anya: Dr. Adelaid.

Polly: Yeah, that was really shocking.

Carole: The one I liked best was Raoul Wallenberg. Did you guys read that one?

Susan: Yeah. I think this one, Dr. Luckner, she was really good.

Polly: I just think . . . Wait, there's some dates in here. It seems it took so long for people to realize, "Oh, God, we have to rescue these people."

Susan: I know.

Polly: I believe that the slowness of the rest of the world . . . I don't understand that.

Anya: What do you mean?

Polly: Why it took that long for the, like, the U.S. . . . . .

Anya: Well, what's written is that the killing didn't really start before we found out about it.

Polly: But the Nazis who killed everybody knew.

Susan: Yeah, it did.

Polly: No, it didn't.

Susan: I guess they wouldn't let anyone out with information. They killed them all.

Carole: Wait. Hold it. Did this one lady, Gertrude, get out? I feel sorry for her.

Polly: The U.S. knew what was happening in 1944, the year that the killing . . . that the Holocaust started.

Anya: Did it just start in 1944? No, that's when it reached a peak.

Polly: No, it started in '44.

Anya: This one, Dr. Adelaid. "That night as she waited for the squad, the German managed to smuggle her . . ."

Carole: She escaped?

Anya: Yeah.

Carole: Part of the concentration camp, wasn't it?

Anya: I don't know if she survived.

Susan: I think what all these people did was really good, but I think it would have been better, instead of for each person to go do something, I think it would have been better for all these people to get together, not that they were in the same place at the same time, but for one person to organize a bunch of people who wanted to go save the Jews. They would have gotten more done with more people together, than just one person.

Carole: Like the one priest who gave his life.

Susan: Yeah, but I think there should have been more of them.

Carole: But it was still hard, cause you've got the Gestapo everywhere. Someone's gonna beep on them, you're gonna tell on them.

Anya: Well, there's not much we can say about this. It's just interesting to hear about. It's just like slavery, you know. It happened, and you hear it.

[extraneous conversation, jokes with neighbors]

Susan: We're back now—

Polly: I thought it was quite interesting and enlightening . . .

Susan: I don't know. I didn't get that much out of it.

Polly: . . . that people would give their own life to save another life.

Susan: Yeah, but so many people died. I think, okay, there were organizations that saved people, right? But why weren't there organizations that fought back to the Nazis and Gestapo?

Anya: They were resisting.

Susan: They were resisting, but not fighting.

Carole: The people in Warsaw fought the Nazis.

Susan: I'm not talking about the Jews; I'm talking about the, you know, the normal people.

Polly: If you heard that they were killing millions of people, what would you do? Actions would be, like . . .

Carole: No way.

Anya: Well, they were all brainwashed anyway.

Susan: I think we should watch, not the "Diary of Ann Frank," but some documentary so we could know what really happened.

As our unit moved along, and we practiced our new procedures, I detected a change in the level of the whole-class discourse. Leading a coherent discussion no longer seemed a struggle. Students listened more to each other and risked revealing themselves; I attributed this to their experience in History Talk Group. On day six the whole class discussed a reading about what happened on *Kristallnacht*. By this time Linda and I were comfortable co-leading the class.

Ms. Brown: Is there anything you'd like to say about this reading? What did you learn from it?

Girl: It sounded like they [Nazis] made up excuses just to kill people or to embarrass them. Like he went to go up to rape her, and she had to wear that sign.

Ms. Brown: Okay.

Girl: I don't think the situation was very surprising. I mean, you would expect people to react like that, especially because they're in fear of their lives. I mean, a lot of people get mad and say, "Why didn't they speak up?" But they couldn't. If only one family in five spoke up, then it'd be easy to kill them, you know. I guess they didn't have any organized . . . not enough people got together and stuff like that . . .

Boy: Did all the people in the Nazi party wear swastikas so that, like, you could identify them? Like your average person?

Ms. Brown: That's a good question.

Ms. Danielson: No, I think you would assume that if they enjoyed full privileges of German citizenship that they were Nazi supporters. He only took away their rights and privileges if they showed resistance. People would assume they were a Nazi supporter, although mentally they might be resisting, but . . .

Girl: Was that woman in a relationship with that Jew?

Another Girl: No, they just said she was.

First Girl: I was wondering, because how can you be in a relationship with someone if he was gonna rape you? It doesn't make sense.

Girl: No, he wasn't gonna rape her.

Girl: No, but that's what they said, right?

Girl: Yeah.

[jumble of voices]

Ms. Danielson: One comment at a time, please.

Girl: Did some Jews get away with . . . they didn't think they were Jews, did they, I mean, change their last names? I mean, were some, I mean, they didn't have to hide, but just act as if they were Germans?

Ms. Brown: Yes, they certainly did. I know a personal history of a Jewish woman who pretended she was Catholic so she could get into medical school in Austria. She succeeded in getting through medical school by passing as Catholic. So that was one option. But most didn't want to erase their identity like that.

Girl: That's understandable.

Ms. Danielson: And some were not able to. If they had been particularly active members of their community, they were known; their names were documented. The synagogues kept records if you had been bar mitzvahed or bat mitzvahed or married or anything. Your names were written down, and they did get hold of that and they knew. There are some people—there's at least one story, and I don't remember the name of the story, but it's in our library, about a woman who disguised the fact that she was Jewish. I think she was actually somewhere in France. And she was successful in hiding the fact that she was Jewish—I think she posed as Catholic probably—for a couple of years, and eventually she falls in love and is about to get married. At that point she had to produce some papers, because it's obvious she's not a French citizen. Somehow, they all find out she was a Jew, and she ended up, instead of getting married, being sent to a concentration camp and being killed there. That's a true story. Karen Peters, the librarian, would know the name of it.

Ms. Brown: Just one final comment. I think you all got it. What is the perspective of this document? Who is writing it?

Girl: It's from a non-Jewish person who is an onlooker, a neighbor. It shows even the non-Jews were affected by the Nazis.

Ms. Brown: Okay, terrific. So if one of you wants to imagine that you are a non-Jewish young person in Germany at this time, trying to figure out what you would do, this story might help you imagine your story.

In retrospect, we felt that we included too little group work because we did not trust the students. We maintained too much control, afraid that students would not be involved enough to work unless we broke everything into little steps and asked everyone to do the same thing at the same time. As Linda commented, "I was still coming from the direction of 'Don't let go.' Now I see we should have let go a little more, a lot more actually, as far as trusting them to read at night and giving them more time to work together."

Because we feared that students wouldn't read our documents unless we had them do it in class, we spent too much classtime reading. We now believe that the documents were powerful enough to grab even the usually disinterested kids and that we could gain classtime for group work by sending more documents home to be read as homework.

Despite the difficulties, I am convinced that History Talk Groups constituted an essential component in carrying out history workshop. They may sometimes seem wasted time, especially to the top grade-earners in class, but much more goes on than meets the eye. With patience and skilled guidance, students can improve their group discussion skills and contribute deeply to one another's thinking. We were less accomplished at this part of history workshop than with the other elements, but we noticeably improved our skills.

Six: Lectures and Class Discussions

These two components I want to analyze together, because they tend to blend into each other. Actually, in our classroom, there seemed to be three categories of class discourse: *lectures*, in which the teacher talked with few comments—usually questions from the students; *chalk-talks*, in which the teacher lectured from an outline on the board with lots of discussion about the meaning of her talk, and *class discussion*, in which a key idea or topic was explored in some depth and from a number of perspectives.

Because I wanted to ascertain at the outset what students wanted to learn about the Holocaust, we did not start by giving information. We eased into our unit, asking questions and discussing fundamental ideas like stereotypes, race, holocaust, anti-Semitism, scapegoating. We read documents and saw a video about Hitler. Students began clamoring for more information. How did Hitler get elected? What did he do to start the war? How did he run his propaganda machine?

During the seventh lesson Linda passed out a one-page chronology covering the years 1915 through 1950, constructed to help students as she lectured. When she talked, students listened intently, finding answers to the questions they had been raising. During the eleventh lesson, Linda spent most of the period lecturing, using the questions from the textbook copied onto the board as a guide. She answered them for students in a most direct, engaging manner, while they could question any aspects they wondered about. This continued for part of lesson twelve—a real departure from the usual apathy with which students usually receive lectures.

Linda and I chose carefully the terms and events essential to understanding Hitler, the Holocaust, and World War II; much had to be omitted. The original list of terms and events that students would have to know included:

- Ideas: genocide, holocaust, race, Jews, Aryans, anti-Semitism, totalitarianism
- Terms: inflation, reparations, Fascism, concentration camps
- Dates/people/events: Treaty of Versailles, Weimar Republic, Adolf Hitler, *Mein Kampf*, *Kristallnacht*, Winston Churchill, Franklin Delano Roosevelt, Allied Powers, Axis Powers, Dachau, Auschwitz, Warsaw Ghetto, Nuremberg Trials, Pearl Harbor, VE Day, VJ Day, Nagasaki and Hiroshima

Lesson fifteen included a fact test straight from the textbook's Teacher's Guide. Students did better than they usually did on similar tests. Lessons seventeen and eighteen were mostly chalk-talks, with another fact and map test in lesson nineteen. About one-sixth of our time was filled with lectures and chalk-talks. Whenever we had a few extra minutes we focused discussion on some of the questions listed on our chart of student-generated questions. We felt satisfied that we had not compromised the dates, facts, names, and terms that our students needed to acquire, and several of the most able ones agreed with this assessment.

A few of our best grade-earners worried whether they were really learning enough. Ruth, in her conference, said she learned most from textbooks, while Erik wondered whether it was to his advantage to spend six weeks on the Holocaust, with only two days on the Holy Roman Empire. I believe this represents a grade anxiety that is very real in today's competition for university and in the competitiveness for grades that students experience in school. However, as these students become accustomed to processing imaginatively the information they are learning, they would come to realize, as Sangeeta did in the course of our unit, how much more they understood and how much better prepared they were, even for standardized tests.

Our third form of class discourse—whole-class, open-ended discussion—served as a way for the class to share ideas and as a model for smaller group discussion. It focused more on ideas than on facts and information, which were brought in as needed. We used whole-class discussion to consider questions like: Who are Jews? What is race? What should have happened to Nazis after their defeat? What other genocides have there been? How should we respond to neo-Nazi groups?

Leading a whole-class, open-ended discussion takes skills different from those used in lectures and chalk-talks. In whole-class
discussions a teacher must listen precisely to what students say,
respond appropriately, and frame provocative questions. This is all
difficult enough to carry off in a two-way conversation; in full class
discussion it has to be done with the whole class in tow. To hold
everyone's attention the teacher must pose questions that engage
students and keep the pace moving, while listening intently. These,
of course, are skills we want to model for our students, so that they
can lead small group discussions effectively.

To lead a class discussion well, a teacher must keep herself, her
opinions, and her knowledge in the background. Like a small group
facilitator, her job is to shape the process to give as many students as
possible a chance to state their knowledge and opinions. This is not
easy to do, especially for teachers accustomed to controlling their
classrooms. When a provocative issue arises, we often cannot resist
inserting our carefully reasoned opinion and demonstrating our vast
knowledge. What young, inexperienced person can then manage to
say a word?

And yet, it is precisely our knowledge—especially about ideas—
that our students need, that they can't invent on their own. History
workshop is a process for provoking their thirst for this knowledge,
but we have to provide the essentials. Our students could not have
made sense of the German Holocaust if we had not started by discussing the ideas of race, genocide, holocaust. One way teachers
deaden history is by omitting ideas and sticking strictly to the
"facts." Ideas are alive and real, and we must include them. An
indispensable guide in this department is Herb Kohl's dictionary of
ideas, *From Archetype to Zeitgeist: Powerful Ideas for Powerful
Thinking* (1992). Kohl wrote this book after teaching college students
and realizing they lacked the basic vocabulary of ideas they needed
for thinking. His book serves secondary teachers and students
equally well.

Seven: The Writing Assignment and Its Process

Since learning history is a process, students need to write to assimi-
late information and figure out how they think and feel about what
happened. The forms in which they write are pedagogical questions
I want to introduce, not resolve.

Writing, if assigned at all in history class, usually occurs in the
form of "reports," also known as research, exposition, or nonfiction.
To vary from the usual and to test my ideas, I decided that a story

would form the major assignment, also known as narrative or fiction. I had no idea whether fifteen year olds could write a story, but based on my earlier experiences with tenth graders, I guessed that they could.

When I introduced this assignment in lesson five, I asked what students knew about the differences between fiction and nonfiction, narrative and exposition, then I filled in where necessary. I gave simple instructions. Students could write about any character in Hitler's Europe between the years 1932 and 1945. Their subjects could be Jewish victims, Nazis, rescuers, German resisters, anything they could think of. I pointed out simply that stories usually have a certain structure: a setting, characterization, a problem or dilemma, rising tension, resolution. I talked a bit about voice, distinguishing between first and third person, and said they could use either. Students had two weeks to think about their character. Linda and I modeled our thinking about the kind of character to write about. We thought that our writing a story, too, would be an important element in helping students. But they got so busy on their own that they never expressed any interest in our stories, and we were only too glad to drop that part of our job. They seemed to have already internalized how to write a story.

In lesson six, students had many questions about their assignment. What voice should they use? "It's your decision," Linda said. What perspective should they take? "You're the author," I replied. They needed to be sure we really meant they could make those decisions themselves. And, of course, they asked, "How long should it be?" "Long enough to tell your story," both of us answered, "maybe five to ten pages."

We added one more requirement—that they include an illustration or a scene from the story that they could portray any way they wished. We thought this would help students describe their character in concrete detail.

Just to review our process, in lesson eight we gave out a worksheet (reprinted in chapter 4) to insure that students were getting on with their stories. In lesson eleven we started writing groups and asked students to discuss their characters with each other for ten minutes. In lesson twelve we collected what we called "the first draft" of their stories. Linda read all of these and commented on them in two nights, so that we could return them during lesson fourteen.

In this lesson we devoted most of the period to a read-around of students' stories. Keeping the same writing groups used in lesson eleven, we asked students to read the other three stories written by their group members and write comments on them.

Five students did not have a story on that day, including Dennis, Erik, and Marie featured in chapter 5. Linda and I asked them to write in class rather than participate in the read-around, since they had nothing to share with their peers. This gave us a chance to conference briefly with them, while the other students were busy reading and writing comments. These brief conferences helped students resolve their blocks and proceed with their stories, except in Marie's case, as described earlier.

Student responses to each other's stories seemed disappointing to us because they were brief. We did not collect them immediately after the class in which they were done, but instead asked the authors of the stories to keep them to help in revisions and then give the student responses to us along with the second draft. Only thirteen made it back to us, and by that time we were too swamped to pay much attention.

Many students, however, reported in their conferences that comments by other students were helpful to them. Now that I have had time to examine my copies of their response sheets, I see that the brief comments are often insightful. Here are a few examples.

Comments for Sangeeta by one student

1. Nina has a Jewish friend; Nina hears about how Jews are inferior and accepts this as fact; talks to her mother; finally reaches a decision.

2. Great ending—the second to last and last paragraphs are especially good and emotional.

3. "I just wanted for it to be as it was." Give more of an explanation. "What if this was only the beginning—a small cramped schoolroom." Confusing. Was it intentional to switch from past to present tense?

4. Where is this taking place? in Germany?

5. Too many commas—rewording some sentences might help. Show more of Nina's thoughts, in the sentence, "I shall have to still think . . ." should be omitted. This would be a good place to add in more of her thought process. She almost seemed to change her mind too quickly.

Comments for Rob by students A and B

1. A Jewish boy who was sent to a concentration camp and sent different places.

   B A Jewish boy who has to live during WW II and live through the hardships of the war

2. A I like the theme and the action.

   B Overall plot of the story, good details.

3. A When everything seems to be going good something bad happens.

   B Should have stated that the boy was Jewish at the beginning.

4. A How is it going to end?

   B Are you ever going to see your parents again?

5. A Make him die.

   B Specific ending.

These represent the first attempt for most of our students at giving constructive feedback on a writing assignment. I am certain that with practice most of them could improve their feedback skills and develop more awareness of what constitutes a good story. Boys and girls might even get their divergent criteria for successful stories into the open. In their evaluations, students from all of Linda's classes said they wanted more time to read and respond to each other's stories.

We collected second drafts three classes following the read-around and the final draft a week later. Over the weekend after the read-around, I realized that we were in trouble with this assignment. Linda and I had too much control and did not trust that students would write unless we set up one guidepost after another. In addition, we were swamped with papers—three versions of twenty-five stories times four classes that Linda teaches.

What to do? Since we couldn't change our instructions in midstream, we were stuck with three drafts. But the future solution was to set aside time for working on stories during class, so that we could monitor students' progress without collecting their papers. If students were busy in class, the teacher could come around to each for a quick, one-to-two minute conference on progress, taking notes on who might need a longer conference at another time. With this system students would forego the benefit of the teacher's written feedback, but would gain brief conferences with the teacher and more peer feedback.

In lesson seventeen, only four days before collecting the final drafts, we added a final requirement to the story. It had to include a preface, in which students explained why they chose their character and described the process they used to develop their story. We added this because we needed this information to understand the stories, and it seemed good practice for next year, when our students would be required to write a preface to their research reports.

Prefaces proved difficult for many students. They were not accustomed to analyzing the perspective of their characters or their own process. But again, this was their first attempt. We felt it was an important element of the assignment and would help them become more self-aware. When we conferenced with them, Linda and I could elicit much more from the students than they could express in a preface. More and better conferences would gradually result in much improved prefaces, as students internalized the dialogue from conferences and learned to do it on their own.

The unit we taught had no time scheduled for individual conferences. On story presentation days, I simply left the class in Linda's hands to hold thirty-minute conferences with selected students. I realized what I learned from them could be crucial when I tried to analyze their stories for writing this book.

The conferences showed me how little the product of an assignment reveals the student's inner processes. Until I conferenced with them, I really had no idea what was going on in their stories, even though I thought I did. In addition, the personal conference validated their work way beyond what a grade could do and confirmed their ownership of their piece. When a teacher listens with respect, students grow.

Therefore, time must be found in class for individual conferences, and teachers must develop the skills for conducting them quickly and effectively. *Conference* seems an appropriate label for my thirty-minute interviews with students, but in class they would be much briefer, talks rather than conferences. There might be one-to-two-minute roving conferences, in which the teacher could get around the whole class in one period, followed later by ten-minute scheduled conferences with those who needed more assistance. In addition, students would be conferencing with one other.

Talking with students about their work is easy, if we can take an attitude of being a curious learner rather than a knowing teacher and set aside our judgments, accepting with intense interest what our young historians have to tell us. Every time students retell their stories they rework them, see the issues clearer, and get closer to identifying the problems.

"Where are you stuck?" usually produces information that helps both the teacher and the writer identify strategies for getting on.

It is important to remember that a teacher's job is not to produce solutions. Students can usually find their own solutions. Our job is to ask questions that help students think. Teachers must also model thinking for them. Each of our questions should be followed by another question until the students see the solution and begin to internalize the questions, so that next time they can ask them of themselves.

Writers of any age are invested in their words and take criticism with difficulty. Teachers need to begin by finding something to commend, then going on to probe with questions. Finding something to commend may be difficult in class, when there is no time to read the whole piece, but teachers can read the lead or the ending. They may ask the student to identify a good, short part of the story for the teacher to read. A quick, light touch is needed, a flick of connection with the student. It can only happen when each student knows she has the teacher's respect.

What follows are the basic questions that I used in my thirty-minute conferences. Just one of them would be enough for a quick talk with a student, for each of these needs to be followed up by several subsidiary questions.

- Please retell your story for me.
- Why did you choose the character you did?
- What helped you the most in writing this story?
- Is there any place where you got really stuck?
- How did you get unstuck?
- How did you work historical information into your story?
- Are there any facts in your story that you wonder whether they are historically accurate?
- Did you appear in your story anywhere?

But how is a teacher to find time for conferencing within the regular class period? The only solution seems to be to schedule more in-class work periods, when students choose from a full range of options what they need to do next. Their options are to draft their story, revise, copyedit, draw, research, read, seek response from classmates, or give response. Meanwhile, the teacher can be conferencing with individual students.

As we taught our unit, Linda and I called this in-class work period "Writing Clinic." We only managed one out of our whole six-week unit, but now we believe that was not nearly enough. We needed several more for checking progress and for conferencing with students.

I would also like to see a final, writing-clinic day scheduled at the end of the unit, after stories are turned in and reviewed by the teacher. On this day the teacher could gather all the students who had major difficulties with mechanics. All those who had few mechanical errors would be free to choose other activities. If many students had similar errors, the teacher could give a minilesson, then hold individual conferences as students worked on their corrections. Alternately, these students could take their stories to English class for assistance in how to correct the mechanical errors.

One final aspect of the writing process needs to be reviewed—illustrations. I included this as a required aspect of the story assignment because I believe that art is essential to thinking and because young students are often greatly assisted in their writing if they draw first, or whenever they get stuck (Jorgensen, 1993). Illustration seems to help students visualize the details they need for writing. I hoped that drawing would help teenagers in the same way, and I wanted to see what would happen if they tried.

Unfortunately, the drawings got swallowed up in the whole process. No one spontaneously mentioned drawing as a help. Every student turned in some kind of illustration, but several were drawn by someone else, which we decided to permit when considerable resistance to this assignment developed and when we remembered that adult writers seldom illustrate their own pieces.

Most of the students felt they were unskilled at drawing and illustrating and were embarrassed by their attempts. Often self-critical, many were not satisfied with the often child-like productions they created. I suspect that the drawings were more valuable to them than students realized. After we pinned the drawings up on the back wall in class, I overheard much discussion going on about them. Next time we would ask for a caption for each one.

So the seven aspects of our experimental unit, then, that seem to be essential features of history workshop are as follows:

1. Concept of history
2. Primary sources
3. Multiple perspectives
4. Journal writing
5. History Talk Groups
6. Lectures and discussions
7. Writing process

Clearly, history workshop is an idea larger than any sum of its components. These are features that Linda and I stumbled on as we made our first attempt at implementing this complex process in a tenth-grade classroom. But no recipe of features will produce history workshop; it can be achieved in a multitude of ways that teachers will invent as it continues to be explored.

Seven

What Next?

Part of the evaluation of history workshop included a careful look at how our experiment affected our students and ourselves. One of our students, Sangeeta, reported that she felt that "many students had been profoundly moved, even though they wouldn't want to admit it."

The students' written evaluations confirmed their positive response, though they fell short—as Sangeeta predicted—of admitting they were profoundly moved. All students liked the writing assignment except Marie, who opposed it on high principle, as explained in chapter 5. Students made suggestions about details that could be improved, but every single one went on record as preferring history workshop to the usual way history is taught.

The school grapevine also brought good news to Linda. Several teachers approached her with questions about history workshop. Many had heard from parents at the Parent Faculty Club, who said their teenagers were loving history class for the first time.

But for Linda the most telling evidence came from a boy in her sixth-period class. She described his response.

> There was one kid in the sixth period on a contract and put in my class this semester because he's a terrible behavior problem. He was going to get kicked out of school. If he does one thing wrong, if he misses any assignment, he's kicked out automatically. [In history workshop] he wrote a story that I thought was good. I was impressed with it; I was impressed mostly that he did it. I was always watching for this kid to mess up, because everyone—the school psychologist, the vice principal, the resource teacher—everyone told me ahead of time, to warn me. Not only has he not made one wrong move, but his paper so impressed all of them (they passed it all around) that

they all came to me to say how impressed they were and how they wanted copies of it. Obviously, it has to be good compared to what he did before. And he's working hard on the new assignment, the country case studies.

The story assignment definitely seems to have helped the D students, the ones who usually don't put out much of anything. "But what about the A students?" I asked Linda. "Was this assignment also productive for them?" She responded:

> I would suspect in some cases they are annoyed because they would rather just be given this rote assignment that they can do very easily, and it's done, and they're successful. On the other hand, they all did really good jobs. I didn't hear anyone say they thought it was a dumb assignment. Everyone said they learned a lot. Some did say, "I think we should have been given more information up front because it would have been easier." I think they felt themselves floundering in the beginning, then they caught on. Because they are used to getting information, they felt uncomfortable not having that.

Linda and I could easily fall into the trap of wanting to reduce the discomfort for the A students. When we heard their complaints, we suggested that maybe next time we would not open with so many questions. Perhaps we could give out more information initially, as we had been doing all our teaching lives.

But some courage is required here. I know in my heart that having to cope with little information is just what the A students needed. Floundering proved productive for them, forcing them out of their passivity into some decision making of their own. With little information provided in the beginning of the unit, the D students participated and the A students were galvanized into real involvement.

And the effect of history workshop on the teachers? I have been "walking on water" with its success, but Linda felt the brunt of the experiment, doing it four times a day. What does she have to say?

> Personally, I learned a lot about myself, and I'm still interested in learning more. I appreciate now that if you really want to know a lot about something, how time-consuming it is. You can't stop asking questions. You have to keep looking different places. It's intriguing. I'm still reading Shirer's *The Rise and Fall of the Third Reich* (1962).
>
> But what I really liked best about history workshop was that the kids liked it so much and the product was *excellent*. It made me feel like a good teacher, with very little effort.
>
> I liked it because it made me take a fresh look at everything I'm doing in all the classes, even the English class. The workshop theory is part of it, but it's also listening to the students. It's amazing, because ever since the idea came in my mind I have been listening

a lot more. I can see their learning much more clearly, more than I could before, just because I'm giving it a chance. I used to have this formula in my mind of how I would get it done. But now I realize everybody's different, and kids have to make their own decisions.

Linda and I have no question that history workshop works in powerful ways, some of which we don't fully understand. But we do know that we want to keep developing it, finding solutions to the difficulties, and enabling our students to make more of their own decisions.

There are five aspects of history workshop that need to be developed as we continue to explore this metaphor for teaching history—organizing the classroom, long-range planning, generating other units, grading, and practicing analytic skills.

Organizing the Room

When I first began to play with the idea of history workshop, I drew room layouts illustrating where extra shelves could be built and how everything could be organized. If 120 to 150 students per day were going to work independently and effectively in one room, I thought, it would have to be 120 to 150 times as well organized as my writing room at home.

When I arranged to co-teach with Linda, I wanted to tell her how we would have to rearrange her room. Good manners stopped me. After all, it was her room, and if I wanted her cooperation I had better figure out how to work in it as it was.

That turned out to be a breakthrough for me, because I learned that history workshop worked just fine without changing anything in the room. Linda had to bring in cardboard boxes to collect all the stories, but that is the only change we made. Her desk did occasionally disappear from view, but that seemed within normal parameters.

The fact is that high school teachers usually think of their room as their space and organize it for themselves. Students use their own desks and not much else. The cabinets and shelves are for the teacher's supplies. This is unlike elementary classrooms, where a teacher may claim a corner for himself, but the rest of the room is organized for children's supplies, resources, and work stations. Elementary teachers usually put great care into making it possible for students to work in their rooms.

While I was working with Linda, she brought into her room many boxes full of old *National Geographic Magazines*, which she planned to have as resources for her students in their next unit. Eventually she got these magazines arranged on the window ledge under the rear windows, standing on the ledge in chronological order. After our unit was finished and Linda was deep into her next unit, I came back for a final talk with her. I found all the bright yellow magazines piled on the floor in disarray under the windows.

"What in the world happened?" I asked.

"Well, the kids used the magazines, all right. But since they had no guide as to how to put them back, they all ended up on the floor."

This story illustrates what high school teachers must learn as they design workshop environments in their classes. If Linda had provided some boxes labeled with dates, her students would have been able to return their *National Geographics* in chronological order ready for the next class to use.

Students in history workshop need access to dictionaries, style manuals, and basic history reference books. Books on the topic under investigation should be available: from the teacher's personal collection, the school library, and other public libraries. These books may circulate if the teacher wants to set up her own card system, or they may be used only in class.

In addition, students may need access to special files of material. For her unit on country reports, Linda provided large boxes with a manila folder on every country being studied, and students could file articles as they found them. These files were available to every class and eventually were filled with materials contributed by all the classes.

Students also each need a file of their own to hold their history writing. At the end of the semester or the year, this portfolio becomes an important tool for reflection, review, and evaluation.

A special place for primary sources is needed. Artifacts and precious photos may need a case that can be locked. Oversized books of photos, tapes and recordings need storage space.

All of this takes care, effort, and time. Most of all, teachers' attitudes must change from, "This room is my workplace" to "This room is a workshop for me and my 150 students."

Long-range Planning

The implementation of history workshop should be seen as a long, slow process. Changes in attitude toward the students and one's conception of history take place over months and years, and there are some basic skills that any teacher needs to have firmly in his repertoire before he is ready to plunge full-scale into attempting history workshop.

The two most important basic skills include working with groups and experience with the writing process. Before beginning history workshop, a teacher can practice cooperative learning in many ways, rehearse how to set up groups, assign the task, have students report out, and debrief the process. Good books and workshops are available for learning these skills, such as David W. Johnson, et al, *Circles of Learning: Cooperation in the Classroom* (1984), and Robert E. Slavin, *Student Team Learning: An Overview and Practical Guide* (1988).

Writing process may be unfamiliar to most secondary history teachers, many of whom have not even taught standard writing. Knowing how to respond to student writing in a helpful way and patiently expecting revisions rather than a finished product in one effort are skills to be practiced. One's peers in the English department can serve as consultants. Again, books and workshops are available. Donald Graves, *Writing: Teachers and Children at Work* (1983), Nancie Atwell, *In the Middle: Writing, Reading and Learning with Adolescents* (1987), and Linda Rief, *Seeking Diversity: Language Arts with Adolescents* (1991), are all excellent places to start.

When one is ready for the first plunge, choose one topic from the semester to teach by history workshop. Use these criteria: What is most interesting to students? What has the most material about it readily available? If this unit goes well, choose another topic to teach by history workshop in the next semester or the next year, after teaching as usual the rest of the time.

An experienced teacher like Linda found history workshop so effective that she did not want to go back to her usual ways. She adapted workshop methods to fit her next unit, *Nationalism in the Modern World*, by scheduling much more workshop time in class than she had previously. For this unit she changed the writing assignment from fiction to nonfiction. Each student produced two reports, one individual and one group, so that again, writing was a major feature of the unit.

Linda was wise to follow a unit based on fiction writing with one featuring a different genre. Fiction seems to especially engage participants and a respite, or distancing, is needed afterwards. The question of how to vary writing assignments systematically in history workshop needs to be addressed if we want students to practice all forms of writing.

Teachers often limit students by offering too few writing genres. Often we choose the very ones that seem most distasteful to students. Possible writing forms include:

Nonfiction	Fiction
poetry	poetry
auto/biography	auto/biography
journals/diaries	journals/diaries
interviews/oral history	interviews/oral history
book reports	historical short stories
reports/short essays	(historical murder mystery,
research/long essays	historical romance)

This list reveals that most genres have both a fictional and non-fictional possibility. The only genres that usually are written solely as nonfiction are book reports and research reports. Students gradually learn these genres by reading and writing them. Sometimes, though not often enough, teachers let students choose what genre they want to read or write; usually, we assign them and our students must practice what we have in mind.

The questions then become, What genres are most valuable? Should students choose their own genres? What sequences is most effective? How should these genres be varied over sixth through twelfth grade? What if English and history faculties actually thought about this question together, instead of relying on random individual choices to accomplish their goals?

In the Victorian era educated people tended to devalue novels. They felt that fiction was unwholesome, not elevating, not educational, mere entertainment of a slightly trashy sort. Perhaps this attitude is still reflected in our history curriculum, with its emphasis on book reports and research reports and its reluctance to encourage fiction, either the reading or the writing thereof.

Students need more encouragement to write in the various fictional genres in grades six through twelve. Research and library skills can be practiced in writing fiction as well as in writing reports. Historical fiction seems a more natural way for many students to put together information until the full development of their logical capacities.

Opportunities and advantages exist for history teachers to work closely with English and Art departments. Since many middle and high schools are currently being restructured to feature two-hour core periods and/or to permit grade coordination by all teachers working with a single grade, these possibilities are becoming real.

In a school that is not yet restructured the history, English, and art departments can simply cooperate in planning. Instead of competing for students' time, departments can reinforce one another's material and enable students to put more time and involvement into core assignments agreed on by all members as most essential and worthwhile.

Other Sample Units

As mentioned, my co-teacher, Linda Danielson, did not hesitate in applying the history workshop method to her next unit, *Nationalism in the Contemporary World*. Her curriculum framework specified that this unit should cover the contemporary period in what used to be the Soviet Union, China, Israel, Syria, Ghana, South Africa, Mexico, and Brazil. For several years Linda had accomplished this by asking her students to produce reports on countries of their choice.

Since Linda had learned in our Holocaust unit to trust students to work on their own, she made a major change in how she structured her unit on country case studies. Instead of walking her students through the unit by having everyone in the class do the same work each period, she made the assignment at the start of the unit and then gave students workshop time to complete the work in the manner they decided was best for them. Each student had two basic assignments—an individual report on one country and a group production of a newspaper about another country. Figure 7-1 shows the sheet Linda gave out to students defining the assignment for them.

This unit lasted the final three months of school. Students worked effectively on their own and in their group for almost a month. Many class periods opened with a ten-minute mini-lesson about aspects of the work with which students seemed to need assistance. They decided how to use the remainder of the period. Often they went to the library. They set up a classroom set of files on each country that all of the classes shared. During the unit Linda reported that: "Kids you wouldn't expect are learning inadvertently, really. The peer mood is, 'We've got to do this. How're you doing on yours? Help me with mine.' I like that. It works. In a workshop environment there isn't anything for kids to do if they aren't participating, because that's what's going on."

During this part of the unit, when Linda had to be away for two days, she left no lesson plan for the substitute except to say, "The students will work. They know what to do." She left a film for the teacher to show in case her students abused their freedom, but they worked diligently with no problems for the sub.

The last six weeks of this unit were devoted to student presentations of their reports, while the rest of the class took notes. Students

Figure 7–1
Country Case Studies Project
(*Total value* = *2,500 possible points*)

Assignment	Value	Due Date
Writing: *1,000 points possible*		
1. Report on the issues in your country. (5–10 pages) Individual project only.	300 points	_____
2. Newspaper. (8–10 articles and graphics) Group project only.	300 points	_____
3. Proposed solution letter to official or editor. This letter will be mailed to the addressee.	300 points	_____
4. Brief history abstract (2–3 pages)	200 points	_____
5. I-Search log	200 points	_____
Graphics: *700 points possible*		
6. Map on poster board.	200 points	_____
7. Depiction of the historical info: time line, story board, scrap book, or comic strip	200 points	_____
8. Graphs & charts. (see info ditto)	300 points	_____
Documentation: *500 points possible*		
9. Note cards	100 points	_____
10. Bibliography cards.	100 points	_____
11. List of work cited (bibliography).	100 points	_____
12. Newspaper analysis portfolio.	200 points	_____
Oral Presentation: *300 points possible*		
13. Precision and range of information	100 points	_____
14. Audience response	100 points	_____
15. Time limit.	100 points	_____

Group due date: _____   Individual due date: _____

were teaching the material to their classmates; Linda could watch. The reports turned out better than those of previous years. Instead of an organization based on categories of geography, education, main products, etc., the reports focused on three or four critical issues in each country, with all the basic economic and geographic facts tied into the issues. This happened, Linda believes, because she followed the history workshop model of opening the unit asking students what questions they had about the countries. The students wanted to know more about the issues in the world. The class brainstormed as Linda wrote their ideas on the blackboard. She left the class-generated issues on the board for weeks as the students thought about the material they were collecting.

By giving students more freedom and responsibility for their own work, Linda lifted their usual constraints. One student produced a college-level report by using Amnesty International reports that she found at a nearby university for source material, while another—who had written an outstanding story during the Holocaust unit—added a short story set in her country. This student was willing to write nonfiction for the assignment, but she had found her favorite genre in fiction.

The history workshop process can work for any topic. The civil rights movement, taught in the eleventh grade in California, offers great potential. After pinning down available primary sources, literary models to use, and the genre of assignment, the actual unit could go in several directions.

One approach could focus on the genre of autobiography. Students might read and write autobiography and oral history, and they might choose to write fictional autobiography, like The Autobiography of Miss Jane Pittman, or to interview a living person about their experiences of the civil rights movement.

A different approach to the civil rights movement would be to choose biography as the genre for the writing project and focus on biographies as the literary model. This provides an opportunity for students to consider the various choices and roles people made and played. Personal accounts can be found from black leaders, black resisters, white supporters, white resisters, northern students who came to help, black children helpers, and martyrs. The writing assignment might be a fictional biography, nonfictional biography, or a choice of either. To help students write biographies, the indispensable guide is Myra Zarnowski, Learning About Biographies (1990).

A third approach to the civil rights movement would be to use it as the general topic for the major research paper of the eleventh grade. In this case every student could choose some aspect of the movement to investigate and write up as a report. Some models of good reportage about the movement would need to be found to guide the students. Taylor Branch, Parting the Waters (1989), is an excellent source. It could be excerpted or portions read aloud, with a bit of photocopying to show how Branch handled the sources and footnotes. Primary sources could be drawn from the wide range of material. Other excellent reference books are described in Appendix B.

As a final example of unit planning, let's look at a middle school topic from California's Framework, "Toward a More Perfect Union (1805–79)." The historical novel, *Across Five Aprils* (1987), by Irene Hunt, works well with this topic. In this novel the Creighton family, on their farm in southern Illinois, becomes involved in the Civil War in April, 1861; the story tells how each member is affected. The writing assignment for this unit could be historical fiction, historical romance, or adventure. Primary sources could include Paul Angle, *A Pictorial History of the Civil War Years* (1980); Milton Meltzer, *Voices from the Civil War* (1990); Milton Meltzer, *The Black Americans: A History in Their Own Words* (1987).

To plan any curriculum unit using history workshop, the following questions need to be asked: What literature is available that links up with the topic? What genres are modeled? What genres do the kids need to practice? What primary sources are available?

Not every unit needs to be taught by the history workshop process. On some topics primary materials will not be available; on others, literary models may not be easily available. If one tried to teach every unit by history workshop, there would not be sufficient time to cover the required curriculum, since the extended writing assignments take more time than is usually allotted. If teachers could use history workshop for just one unit each semester, students would benefit greatly. In other units ground can be covered faster with the usual shorter writing assignments and short-answer tests.

However, even if we teachers are not quite ready for a full history workshop, students may well be. When high schools enroll students who are accustomed to writing process in elementary and middle school, they may request writing projects as a way to think about history. They won't be content with just one draft. Our students may bring workshop along with them.

Grades and Assessment

The methods of grading that Linda and I used in our unit seem far from exemplary. We did not attempt to change this area of our work and simply did what we've always done. Linda gave the grades in our Holocaust unit and got me off the hook. She felt that without the incentive of points and grades many of the students would not produce the work in a timely fashion.

Current grading procedures must be reconsidered when using the history workshop process. Most students will work without the incentive of grades on each minor part of work. The boys making D in Linda's class began to work when we changed the assignment, not because of grades. Everyone turned in an illustration, though we gave no points for them.

Setting high standards and helping students learn to analyze and assess their own progress toward those standards is part of the history workshop process. Many students have learned to think of intelligence as a fixed and single entity—you succeed or fail depending on how "smart" you are. Assignments and assessments need to be changed so that students can discover, on the contrary, that most achievement results from a succession of corrected mistakes that is part of a long process of hard work. That's why extended writing assignments and portfolio assessment make sense.

Since Linda's students had never even participated in writer's response groups before, we were starting from scratch with them. Although they accepted process as a way of doing things, we didn't have time to help them develop their own criteria for effective historical writing. In their discussions with us and with each other, and in their final interviews with me, they laid the foundations for creating such criteria. The ideas were all in their minds; we needed only to take part of a class period to develop the list with them. Had we done so, I think the class would have produced something similar to this:

Characteristics of Effective Historical Fiction

- lead—grabs attention and gives direction to what is to come
- middle—organized, logical, clear, lots of action (boys), relationships clear and developed (girls)
- ending—brings piece to a close satisfactorily
- characters—understandable, believable, complex
- appeals to reader—reader can relate and stay interested
- style—lots of description, fresh words
- accuracy—details are historically correct; names and places are accurate; no anachronisms
- mechanics—legible writing; correct spelling, punctuation and paragraphing

Linda Rief, in her work in language arts with eighth graders, has carried the assessment process forward in the way it should move in historical writing. Rief creates three components for the grade instead of the two we used; hers are process, content, and mechanics. She invites the students to grade themselves in all three categories and then explain their grades; on the same grading sheet, she gives her grade in each category with her comments. In this way Rief connects students' own evaluation of themselves with the normative standards that she, the teacher, used in comparing their work to that of a larger sample of students (1991).

Students can, over time, internalize high standards of historical thinking and writing through a process of developing the criteria, reading excellent models, and analyzing their own work and the work of their peers. This process requires more skill and patience on the part of teachers than short-answer tests do, but once we see how students flourish under writing process and portfolio assessment, how can we turn back? Of course, history teachers may always want to give map quizzes and short-answer identification questions to check for basic factual information. But process assessment of history writing skills must also become part of our repertoire.

Analytic Skills

This text emphasizes one end of the continuum of the historical skills—those of imagination and empathy, rather than those of critique and analysis. I have not dealt here with expository writing—constructing an argument in the form of a report or essay. Secondary students do need to practice constructing arguments, but not to the exclusion of narrative construction, which most of them seem to find much easier and more natural. Thus, to complete the idea of history workshop, the whole area of argumentation needs to be examined in the context of what skills, exercises, and genres are appropriate for adolescents in public school.

The transformation of the disciplines of history and English during the last quarter-century has meant that the basic skills of the humanities have also been transformed. Whereas the emphasis used to be on describing individuals and trends within cultures measured in short time periods, now the skills required are cultural analysis and comparison over longer time periods. The big questions to be answered are how does culture work and how does it change?

This revolution in the humanities is still underway, of course, and the new synthesis has not yet fully emerged from the battles between the canonists and the innovators. But a way to the new synthesis has been outlined by Peter N. Stearns in *Meaning over Memory: Recasting the Teaching of Culture and History* (1993).

Stearns proposes a humanities workshop for high schools to be conducted three or four days of every two-week unit, with the same purpose as science laboratory—to introduce the basic methods of the discipline. He suggests that exercises in humanities workshop could start by asking students to build an argument from one or two primary sources, then move to building arguments focused on a pre-set analytical question using more complex collections of sources. Finally, students could confront diverse interpretations and the structure of argument itself. By eleventh grade, he urges, some specific comparative problems could be introduced to wean students away from oversimple assumptions about single cultures. For these problems he suggests comparative analysis of slavery, or why the United States produced so little socialism compared to Europe, topics on which materials are currently available.

The sequence of how students learn to write effective exposition needs to be carefully considered by teachers. Doing it as we have always done it is not enough. Our students have changed; our culture, our scholarship, and our relationship to the rest of the world has changed. The opportunity has never been greater to modify what happens in secondary school.

The Teacher's Attitude

Whatever the skills being practiced, whatever the genre, whatever the procedure for assessment or the room arrangement, the most important ingredient in history workshop lies in the teacher's attitude toward the students. Linda had her finger on it when she said to me after our unit was complete: "You know, you kept saying, 'Let's listen to the students, listen to the students.' I think I've finally got it. I'm hearing lots more now."

So often teachers see students as objects to be sorted into the appropriate categories A, B, C or D, depending on how close they get to the right answers in class and on tests. Teachers control the questions and the right answers, and students who want high grades try their best to figure out what is in the teacher's mind.

Since I have survived as a classroom teacher, I have been able to function in this way, too. But my underlying attitude arises out of a different set of metaphors. I see students as actors on the vast stage of life, and as I approach each one I think, "Now, who do we have here?" I value them all; I know that the great human play, the strut of people across the stage, can't go on properly without every single role being filled. I love being in public schools, because they are the complete Central Casting. There I find one of every imaginable person—young and fresh from the mint, just becoming aware of who they are.

I don't want to sort students into similar categories, but to differentiate them, revealing the nuances of character and talent unique to each one. Then, out of the amazing assemblage of the idiosyncratic and the incomparable we can create a powerful play together.

This is too self-evident to belabor, except to correlate it with conditions in a high school classroom. Relating personally and with clarity to 150 individuals every day presents a complex challenge to secondary teachers. Most of us do not even attempt it; we protect ourselves behind the procedures customary in classrooms.

History workshop is a way to treat each class of thirty kids as if they were our only thirty that day. It is a way to teach students that learning history is a continuous process, a way to listen to kids, to empower them through recognition of their special qualities. Finally, it is a way to teach them the history they need to know to take a productive role in it.

Appendix A

Additional Samples of Student Writing

This is the story written by Sam, the pen name chosen by the one Jewish student in our class, a girl. Sam makes average grades, sits in a front-row seat, and takes a quiet part in class.

The Journal of Francis Miller
March 5, 1940

Dear Journal,

I am so happy I just got my new journal for my 16th birthday. well since you no nothing about me I'll tell you; I'm about five feet four inches. I have brown hair, green eyes and fair skin. I am not considered fat but I am sure I could lose a few pounds. Oh my gosh, I almost forgot, my full first name is Francis Miller, Fran for short. My family is considered to be a middle class Jewish family. I was born in Germany on March 5, 1924. Well it's lights out, goodnight.

March 6, 1940

Dear Journal,

Today while I was in the market selling some bread and eggs to Mr. Longridge at the very fair price of $25 [which is a good price for the black market]. I met his son Sol. He is very handsome and is a Polish solder. the good news is that Sol is going to come over for dinner, I don't think he knows that I'm Jewish, I sure hope he doesn't get upset about it. Well he's here. goodnight.

March 7, 1940

Dear Journal,

What a wonderful night. Sol is so interesting and he doesn't mind us being Jewish because he is to and he hides it so well. Now some bad news- the market was cleared out today and over 200 people were arrested for not having their proper papers. I am so glad I was home when this happened. Sol said that he could get me some papers so I can't be arrested. Goodnight!

March 8, 1940

Dear Journal,

I hate this day I wish it had never happened. two very bad things happened today, for starters over the past 3 days 400,000 people were moved into a ghetto in Warsaw. It was terrible they came to our house and told us to get into the truck to leave for Warsaw we have a 2 bedroom house for 8 eight people which is better than some have it but I hate it. The second thing that happened was I found out that Sol was captered by the Germans and put into a labor camp in Poland called Plaszow. It's so terrible I miss him so much. To make things worse I think I'm pregant.

May 1, 1940

Dear Journal,

Well today I went to the doctor and found out that I am 3 months pregant. This is terrible I don't think I'm going to make it another 6 months. Well the good news is that I got a letter from Sol today it says:

Dear Francis, sorry for making you go through this. Well, that's all I have to say for today. I love you. Sol
Isn't that sweet.
P.S. life in the ghetto stinks, we are restricted to what we do. I'm so bored! Goodnight.

January 5, 1941

Dear Journal,

Well its been a long time since I've written, a lot has happened over this period of time. I had my baby on November 8, 1940 it was a boy I named him after his father. other good news is that Sol and I are getting married when he gets home which I hope is soon I miss him so much. Well lets see more buses and trucks come to take people to Auschwitz, thank god none of my family has gone. I don't think I could handle any of my family ever leaving me. Goodnight!

April 10, 1942

Dear Journal,

It's been a long time since I've written you but I haven't had a moment to spare, so please forgive me. Anyway, today I was in town with Sol jr. who is almost 2 years old. He is growing so much. Anyway, the Nazi police came and arrested people even if they had their papers. Sol jr. and I barely escaped with our lives. I hope this war ends soon because I can't keep running in case the Nazis try to take them away. I sure hope they don't have to use them. I am scared I don't want to die. I'll do anything not to die. Goodnight!

March 28, 1943

Dear Journal,

Today was horrible if I didn't have Sol jr. I would kill myself. When Sol returned from Poland at about 3am. He tried to sneak weapons into the ghetto and was shot down in front of everyone and used as an example to other Jews who try to stop the Nazis from taking over. The sad thing is that I never saw him. I loved him so much. Goodnight!

April 2, 1943

Dear Journal,

Today the Nazi's came and took 300,000 people to Auchwitz, by putting people into trucks and trains, but 60,000 of us fought off the soilders with the weapons we had. My family is gone, it is now just me Sol jr. My job is to take care of the injured and hide people in the tunnels we built. The tunnels are full of water and getting people through is difficult but has to be done. It is great knowing that I am helping my fellow Jews. Goodnight!

April 16, 1943

Dear Journal,

I better go back out and fight! I hope this war ends soon, I can't take this much longer.Living in these tunnels is hard, we hardly have any food and things don't look good. Goodnight!

May 1, 1943

Dear Journal,

Today we lost a lot of men I don't think we will last much longer. Today I sent Sol jr. away to Sweden to live with a friend. Hopefully he will survive this war, so maybe he'll survive this war. Goodbye! Francis Miller age 19.

EPILOGUE [*This was written by Sol jr.*]

My mother and 60,000 other people were killed when the Nazis burned the getto down. To make sure no one survived. Little did they know I survived. My mother has always wanted people to know that not all Jewish people were silent witnesses.

Isn't that wonderful for an average student? I didn't find time to ask Sam about her difficulties with spelling and punctuation. Perhaps she made mistakes to simulate diary entries! As the only Jewish student in this class, Sam wrote in her evaluation that she "learned more about where I came from and how my ancestors used to live. I've always loved history, and this just made it more interesting."

To avoid the impression that all the boys who were barely getting by suddenly blossomed into studious, hardworking, reflective beings, I include this story by Hosh, who sits on the back row and joshes a lot:

Hitler and I

My name is Adam Weichdreig. I'm six foot, two inches and I weigh about 200 pounds. I am a German soldier. Actually a bodyguard for the one and only Adolf Hitler. Yaaa, the one and only butthead. My mother always told me that I was a survivior. I know how to kiss up and obey those above you. Even those whom I don't necessarily like at all. I am trying to get close to Hitler. I am trying to make him like me. All those speeches of his didn't fool me. The guy is a scam artist and if I had my way, I would kick his butt and then make him die suffering. Before I do that, I have to get close to him both emotionally and physically. All I have to do is just pretend that I think like him and pretend that we have a lot of things in common. The only thing we have in common is that we are both scaming to kill someone, only he is planning to kill a whole race, which I would not do unless there were a whole race of people named Hitler that hated everyone but Germans.

The day that I became a Nazi was the day Hitler killed my parents. He killed them because they stood against him. Now I'm his bodyguard. I can't wait to get him back.

It's 1940 and I'm in Hitler's bedroom. He is writing down all the different things he could do to people in concentration camps. He's a sick man because he does this when he is bored. It is funny though because he is thinking of all the different things he's going to do to those poor people, and I'm thinking of different ways I could kill him!

When the great Americans finally win this war I'm going to do something he does. Trick him. I'm going to bring him to safety or at least that's what he'll think and then surprise him with torture, then death. He doesn't even know how bad I want to kill him. Never will I show mercy for him. Never. Of coarse he doesn't know that.

FOUR YEARS LATER

"Ahhhhhhh!", screamed Hitler as he screamed some more. He was really mad because just like I thought the U.S. was winning the war and had just defeated Germany. Hitler was so mad. Then he heard that people were set out to kill him all over Europe. So he turned to me and said, "You still like me don't you?" in German. I told him "Yes!!" He told me that we should get to safety and I knew where to go, so I brought him down to one of those bunkers. We could hear all the bombs dropping all around us, each one aiming toward Hitler. I finally got him to the point which I had been waiting for. He thought he was going to be safe and so did his latest wife who I thought was ugly. I sat him down to talk to him. I told him what he did to my parents. He was begging for forgiveness. He was going to commit suicide but I wouldn't give him the pleasure. I felt I had earned the pleasure of killing him. I experienced the greatest feeling in the world. There is no feeling like the feeling that you get when you punch Adolf Hitler right smack dab in the mouth. I began to beat the crud out of him. You could see blood oozing out of his mouth and nose. I had cut him with a razor sharp knife in many places all over his body. I sprinkled salt all over his open wounds and then salt water. I poured some bleach on all his cuts and scrapes. Then after all that fun stuff I burned him alive in one of those ovens. I told German soldiers that he committed suicide and together we got rid of the ashes. Then the bombs came again and what do you know but one falls on me. At least I went out in style!

In his evaluation Hosh wrote: "I learned more and got to write a pretty weird story. It was sooooo much better [than using the textbook]." He recommended applying our method to "all the wars," gave the writing assignment a score of seven out of ten, and felt he didn't learn anything about himself that he didn't already know.

To make comparisons with the girls' stories, here is the story of Erik, the sole boy with an A− average going into this unit:

Experiences of a Nazi Executioner: A Mini-Historical Novel
The Journal of John B. Schwortzchov

My Life

My name is John B. Schwortzchov. I was born in Berlin, Germany on April 12, 1908. I grew up with my mother and father. As an able-bodied Caucasian Roman Catholic male, I was recruited for the German army during World War I, and recently for Hitler's Third Reich Army, where I received numerous medals of honor. My worldwide travels taught me many languages including English, French, Spanish, Russian, Latin, Greek, Italian, Polish, Chinese, Korean, and Japanese, in addition to my native German.

Today in 1942 I serve the state as a Lieutenant in the Nazi Army.

My First Day

January 18, 1942—The sound of the bugle broke the cold winter morning in Southeast Poland. This was my first day off the battlefield and my first day as a guard in a Nazi concentration camp. I rose from my small bed and began preparing for breakfast.

In Auschwitz not everyone ate together. Actually, that was somewhat of an understatement. Prisoners did not eat with the guards. Not even all the guards ate together. The higher ranking officers ate first, while the others stood guard. Then they switched. The military officers got first choice of food, and the prisoners got what little burned refuse was left over.

The large mess hall in which we ate contained close to a hundred tables. A huge Nazi flag hung over the serving line.

Breadfast, I was told, used to begin with a prayer. Recently, however, the prayer had been replaced by singing the national anthem and saluting a statue of Fuhrer, Adolf Hitler.

The food there was not as good as I was used to back in Berlin, but it was better than the battlefield rations. The war had limited the amount of food available, and what little we did have the military chefs almost always burned. Items like chocolate were so rare many people hadn't seen them since the war began.

After I finished eating, I reported to building 85B to receive my orders. The building, like most others in the camp, was grey and plain. The entire camp was surrounded by three rows of chain linked fences with barbed wire along the top. Between each there were dogs. Dogs were not usually out, but when a prisoner attempted to escape, the dogs were ruthless on their victims. As I walked in the door, I heard someone.

"Lieutenant Schwortzchov?" a voice asked.

"Hail Hitler!", I answered with an arm salute.

"Hail Hitler!", he responded. "I am Colonel Garamachov. Today you begin your new assignment."

He abruptly stopped and looked at me. I stood at attention. He then turned around and began walking in circles around his desk. He continued. "You are to assist with the Jewish extermination."

"Yes, sir," I replied. This was a position I had wanted for many years. I wanted to serve my nation since I was a boy. Now, I would have my chance to eliminate the traitorous Jews for the good of the German people.

"You are excused."

I saluted, about faced, and returned to the barracks. Before falling asleep I read fifty pages of my favorite book, *Mein Kampf*.

Rumors Spread

I woke up the next morning eager to get started on the elimination of Germany's problems. I could taste the blood.

As I walked into building 85A, I noticed the room had two desks, a radio, and a door leading into what appeared to be a large showering room. I wondered if I was in the correct building. Just then, Colonel Garamachov opened the door behind me.

"Good morning Lieutenant."

"Hail Hitler!" I promptly responded

"Hail Hitler!" the colonel repeated. "Allow me to introduce my assistant Lieutenant Colonel Aminochen."

I promptly saluted my superior officer without saying a word.

"Bring in the first batch of prisoners," Colonel Garamachov ordered.

As Lieutenant Colonel Aminochen and I separated the strong prisoners from the weak ones, I felt him put his arm around my shoulder. Confused, I pushed it off.

"Don't you like me?" he asked.

"What are you talking about?" I demanded angrily. "Are you some kind of homosexual?"

He didn't say anything, but I could tell from his facial expression he was one.

"If you don't cooperate with me, I can cause you a lot of problems." Aminochen threatened.

"I'm not interested," I asserted firmly.

"You'll regret that decision," Aminochen promised.

Later that night at dinner, people were talking about a Jew who infiltrated the guards. After asking around, I discovered Lieutenant Colonel Aminochen had started the rumor.

My reward

It started out as an ordinary, cloudy day in Auschwitz. After breakfast I reported to building 85A. Colonel Garamachov was particularly quiet this morning. I was used to the executions now. The deaths were no longer emotional for me. I just sipped my coffee and continued with business as usual.

After the last three batches of Jewish prisoners had been eliminated, the Colonel finally spoke.

"Lieutenant Schwortzchov, would you like that man's watch?" the colonel inquired, pointing at a gold watch on one of the dead Jews. This was not unusual, since officers often looted the dead bodies for jewelry.

"No, Sir," I replied firmly.

"Then I wish to have it. Bring it to me," the Colonel demanded.

I set down my coffee and stepped inside the gas chamber. The walls were plain blue tile, but I could see more. I saw the suffering of every man, woman, and child who had ever entered this room. I saw children screaming out as their parents collapsed to the floor. I saw men watching helplessly as life was sucked out of their wives.

I kneeled down by the man. His long, dark beard attached to his lifeless face. I raised his arm, and laid it on my knee, and began to unfasten it from his limp arm. I released his arm and held the golden watch in the palm of my hand. I stood up and began walking to the door.

Just then I saw the Colonel and two other men closing the door. My pace hastened but the door was firmly locked before I could reach it.

Green gas began to ooze from the ceiling. I could feel my chest begin to expand and contract more rapidly. The face of every Jew that had ever died here flashed before my eyes. For the first time in my life, I began to think death by poison gas was cruel and unusual. Now experiencing it myself, I realized the Jews I saw die were really people.

Suddenly, everything went blank. I fell to the floor. The cold tile floor pressed against my face. Then silence.

Erik, a handsome, bespeckled young man, sits halfway back at the right edge of class. He contributes regularly to class discussions and works on the school newspaper outside of class.

Erik told us his story is about a German who felt he needed to serve his country. Erik thinks he "probably could have written about a Jewish character, but there was so much being said about Jews that I felt I should concentrate on the other parts of the Nazi policies."

Erik realized that the nationalism of his character represented a part of himself. Erik grew up in the Cold War period as the son of an Air Force officer. "Even as a kid I was affected by propaganda and the feeling that when I grow up I have to do something for my country. And that's what the main character in my story felt. I haven't given up that feeling entirely, but my feelings toward governments have changed since then. I don't really identify with any government now. I kind of identify with nongovernment, no form of authority, almost anarchy. I'm a teenager so that's normal, I guess."

Erik chose a Nazi "to show that you're not necessarily safe even if you belong to the Nazi party." He decided to have his character get killed, for at first he thought "it would be cool to write all the gory stuff about his death." But then he realized that he wanted to create "some kind of change rather than having some guy who just goes along and nothing happens to him, because that would be boring."

Before choosing the homosexual advance as the way his characer would get into trouble, Erik considered having a black soldier try to be friends with Lt. Schwortzchov, who would be too racist to accept his friendship. Mike wrote his first draft this way, then realized it wasn't a good idea when he thought, "What would a black guy be doing in a Nazi concentration camp?"

Erik says that homosexuality is not something he knows much about, but since the Nazis went after homosexuals, which he learned about in class, he thought of this as a way that Lt. Schwortzchov could be tricked into his own death.

Erik didn't do any research outside of class. He relied on the class handouts to give him details about how the gas chambers worked. He didn't talk to friends or family about his story, except to ask a friend who has bookshelves of photo books about this period to copy about twenty photos, from which Erik chose one for his artwork. He used a scanner on his computer to reproduce it. He did not look at the books themselves; he felt that would be too overwhelming.

Erik, it turns out, has a serious interest in writing, as expressed in his work on the school newspaper. His father was a sports writer for several newspapers. Erik felt that he got the details of his story well at the beginning and end, with almost nothing in the middle. That was the part he had to work on. He said he didn't do as many drafts as usual for him; he just got rid of the sudden jump in the middle and extended the detail a bit. Erik also had to work on the dates. Linda pointed out on his first draft that he started his story in 1938, before the Nazi concentration camps were really in force. Erik wasn't thinking about dates while he was writing the story, but once he had the story he could get the dates accurate, and in the process clarified the march of events for himself.

According to Erik, he "learned a lot about a narrow area, but I wonder if that's really to my benefit to learn so much about—it almost just blew the Holocaust out of the proportions of the entire history of the world, spending a month or more on it. The Holocaust only lasted five years. The Roman Empire lasted for much longer than that, and we spent two days on it."

As a son of the military, Erik was aware of all the aspects of World War II that we did not cover—the Eastern front, the war itself, the politics of war, how it affected the home front. Whose history will it be, indeed?

Appendix B

Sources of Primary and Literary Documents

Adamson, Lynda G. 1987. *A Reference Guide to Historical Fiction for Children and Young Adults.* Westport, CT: ARH/Greenwood Publishing Group.

Bell, Susan G., and Karen M. Offen, eds. 1983. *Women, the Family and Freedom: The Debate in Documents.* vol. 1, 1750–1850; vol. 2, 1850–1950. Stanford, CA: Stanford University Press.

Carey, John, ed. 1987. *Eyewitness to History.* New York: Avon.

Documentary Photo Aids, Inc., P.O. Box 956, Mount Dora, FL 32757. (904) 383-8435. Sets of 11-inch by 14-inch black-and-white photographs printed on cover stock about many important historical topics. Send for free catalog.

Howard, Elizabeth F. 1988. *America As Story: Historical Fiction for Secondary Schools.* Chicago, IL: American Library Association.

Jackdaws. Sixty-five collections of primary sources by topic; forty-two topics in U.S. history, twenty-three in world history. Jackdaws Publications, P.O. Box A03, Amawalk, NY 10501. (914) 962-6911.

Lessons of the Vietnam War: A Modular Textbook. 1988. Pittsburgh, PA: Center for Social Studies Education.

Literature for History-Social Science, Kindergarten Through Grade Eight. 1991. Sacramento, CA: California Department of Education.

Meltzer, Milton. 1987. *The Black Americans: A History in Their Own Words 1619-1983.* Rev. ed. New York: HarperCollins Children's Books.

Meltzer, Milton. 1991. *Rescue: The Story of How Gentiles Saved Jews in the Holocaust.* New York: HarperCollins Children's Books.

Meltzer, Milton. 1990. *Voices From the Civil War.* New York: HarperCollins Children's Books.

Ravitch, Diane, ed. 1990. *The American Reader: Words That Moved a Nation*. New York: HarperCollins.

Recommended Literature, Grades Nine Through Twelve. 1989. Sacramento, CA: California State Department of Education.

Reese, Lyn and Jean Wilkinson, eds. 1987. *Women in the World: Annotated History Resources for the Secondary Students*. Metuchen, NJ: Scarecrow Press.

"The Red Scare of 1919-1920," plus fifteen other titles in U.S. history and fifteen in world history, spiral-bound sourcebooks about fifty pages each. National Center for History in the Schools, University of California-Los Angeles, Moore Hall 231, 405 Hilgard Avenue, Los Angeles, CA 90024-1521.

Watts, J.F. and Allen F. Davis. 1983. *Generations: Your Family in Modern American History*. 3rd ed. New York: Alfred A. Knopf.

Works Cited

Angle, Paul. 1980. *A Pictorial History of the Civil War*. New York: Doubleday.

Atwell, Nancie. 1987. *In the Middle: Writing, Reading and Learning with Adolescents*. Portsmouth, NH: Boynton/Cook.

Bradley, N.C. 1947. "The Growth of the Knowledge of Time in Children of School-Age." *British Journal of Psychology*, 38, 67-68.

Branch, Taylor. 1989. *Parting the Waters: America in the King Years 1954–1963*. New York: Simon and Schuster.

Chaikin, Miriam. 1992. *A Nightmare in History: The Holocaust 1933–1945*. Boston: Houghton Mifflin.

Chartock, Roselle and Jack Spencer. 1978. *The Holocaust Years: Society on Trial*. Anti-Defamation League.

Dewey, John and Evelyn Dewey. 1915. *Schools of Tomorrow*. New York: E.P. Dutton.

Downey, Matthew T. and Linda S. Levstik. 1991. "Teaching and Learning History," in *Handbook of Research on Social Studies Teaching and Learning*. James P. Shaver, ed. pp. 400–410. New York: Macmillan.

Egan, Kieran. 1979. *Educational Development*. New York: Oxford University Press.

Egan, Kieran. 1990. *Romantic Understanding: The Development of Rationality and Imagination. Ages 8–15*. New York: Routledge.

Egan, Kieran. 1986. *Teaching as Storytelling: An Alternative Approach to Teaching and the Curriculum*. Chicago: University of Chicago Press.

Frank, Anne. 1985. *Anne Frank: The Diary of a Young Girl*. New York: Pocket Books of Simon and Schuster.

Gaines, Ernest J. 1982. *The Autobiography of Miss Jane Pittman*. New York: Bantam.

Gardner, Howard. 1992. *The Unschooled Mind: How Children Think and How Schools Should Teach*. New York: Basic Books.

Gilbert, Martin. 1969. *Jewish History Atlas*. Rev. ed. New York: Macmillan.

Gilligan, Carol, Nona P. Lyons and Trudy J. Hanmer, eds. 1989. *Making Connections: The Relational Worlds of Adolescent Girls at Emma Willard School*. Cambridge, MA: Harvard University Press.

Goodlad, John I. 1984. *A Place Called School: Prospects for the Future*. New York: McGraw-Hill.

Graves, Donald H. 1983. *Writing: Teachers and Children at Work.* Portsmouth, NH: Heinemann.

Hallam, R.N. 1967. "Logical Thinking in History." *Educational Review.* 19, 183-202.

Hallam, R.N. 1972. "Thinking and Learning in History." *Teaching History.* 2, 337-346.

"The Hiding Place." 1975. (Video). Directed by James F. Collier. Rev. Billy Graham's Evangelistic Association.

"Hitler: Portrait of Tyranny." Narrated by Hal Holbrick, written by Harriet Lane, edited by David Hansen. Arthur Holch and Candy Kresky, executive producers.

Hitler, Adolf. 1986. *Mein Kampf.* Newport Beach, CA: Noontide Press. First published in two vols., 1925-27.

History-Social Science Framework for California Public Schools Kindergarten Through Grade Twelve. 1988. Sacramento, CA: California Department of Education.

Holt, Tom. 1990. *Thinking Historically: Narrative, Imagination, and Understanding.* New York: College Entrance Examination Board.

Hunt, Irene. 1987. *Across Five Aprils.* New York: Berkley Publishers.

Johnson, David W. et al. 1984. *Circles of Learning: Cooperation in the Classroom.* Alexandria, VA: Association of Supervision and Curriculum Development.

Jones, Ron. 1981. "The Wave." Video teleplay by Johnny Dawkins, based on the short story by Ron Jones. Directed by Alex Grafhos. T.A.T. Communications Co.

Jorgensen, Karen L. 1993. *History Workshop: Reconstructing the Past with Elementary Students.* Portsmouth, NH: Heinemann.

Jorgensen, Karen. 1988. *New Faces of Liberty.* San Francisco: Zellerbach Family Fund.

Jorgensen, Karen and Cynthia Stokes Brown. 1992. *New Faces in our Schools: Student Generated Solutions to Ethnic Conflict.* San Francisco: Zellerbach Family Fund.

Jorgensen-Esmaili, Karen. 1988. "Another Look at Community History," in *History in the Schools: What Shall We Teach?* Bernard Gifford, ed. New York: Macmillan.

Klee, Ernest, Willi Dresser and Volker Riess, eds. 1988. *'The Good Old Days': The Holocaust as Seen by Its Perpetrators and Bystanders.* Translated by Deborah Burnstone. New York: Free Press.

Kohl, Herbert. 1992. *From Archetype to Zeitgeist: Powerful Ideas for Powerful Thinking.* Boston: Little, Brown & Co.

Lowry, Lois. 1990. *Number the Stars.* New York: Dell.

Matas, Carol. 1991. *Lisa's War.* New York: Scholastic, Inc.

Meltzer, Milton. 1987. *The Black Americans: A History in Their Own Words 1619-1983.* Rev. ed. New York: HarperCollins Children's Books.

Meltzer, Milton. 1977. *Never to Forget: The Jews of the Holocaust.* New York: Dell.

Meltzer, Milton. 1991. *Rescue: The Story of How Gentiles Saved Jews in the Holocaust.* New York: HarperCollins Children's Books.

Meltzer, Milton. 1990. *Voices From the Civil War.* New York: HarperCollins Children's Books.

Novick, Peter. 1988. *That Noble Dream: The "Objectivity Question" and the American Historical Profession.* New York: Cambridge University Press.

Oakden, E.C. and Sturt, M. 1922. "The Development of Knowledge of Time in Children." *British Journal of Psychology.* 12, 309-336.

Plant, Richard. 1986. *The Pink Triangle: The Nazi War Against Homosexuals.* New York: Henry Holt & Co.

Rief, Linda. 1991. *Seeking Diversity: Language Arts with Adolescents.* Portsmouth, NH: Heinemann.

Rogasky, Barbara. 1988. *Smoke and Ashes.* New York: Holiday House.

Selzer, Michael. 1978. *Deliverance Day: The Last Hours at Dachau.* Philadelphia: Lippincott.

Sender, Ruth Minsky. 1986. *The Cage.* New York: Bantam Books.

Shirer, William L. 1962. *The Rise and Fall of the Third Reich: A History of Nazi Germany.* New York: Crest Books.

Slavin, Robert E. 1988. *Student Team Learning: An Overview and Practical Guide.* Rev. ed. Washington, DC: National Education Association.

Spiegelman, Art. 1991. *Maus: A Survivor's Tale.* vols. 1–2. New York: Pantheon.

Stearns, Peter N. 1993. *Meaning Over Memory: Recasting the Teaching of Culture and History.* Chapel Hill, NC: University of North Carolina Press.

Steinbeck, John. 1970. *Of Mice and Men.* New York: Bantam Books.

Stoskopf, Allen. "Examining Historical Roots of Racism and Anti-Semitism." Two parts. *Facing History and Ourselves News.* (Fall 1991, Spring 1992).

Strom, Margot Stern and William S. Parsons. 1982. *Facing History and Ourselves: Holocaust and Human Behavior.* Watertown, MA: Intentional Educations, Inc.

Terkel, Studs. 1984. *The Good War: An Oral History of World War II.* New York: Pantheon.

Uhlman, Fred. 1986. *Reunion.* New York: Penguin.

Wiesel, Elie. 1989. *Night.* New York: Bantam Books.

Zarnowski, Myra. 1990. *Learning About Biographies: A Reading and Writing Approach for Children.* Urbana, IL: National Council of Teachers of English.

Zuckerman, Yitzhak. 1993. *Surplus of Memory: Chronicle of the Warsaw Ghetto Uprising.* Berkeley, CA: University of California Press.

Also available from Heinemann . . .

Constructing Buildings, Bridges, and Minds
Building an Integrated Curriculum Through Social Studies
Katherine A. Young, Boise State University

Constructing Buildings, Bridges, and Minds introduces and guides
teachers through the process of using major classroom projects
to facilitate integration of the curriculum. As the author describes
the energy and excitement that fills her classroom during the
Washington, D.C. and Latin America projects, readers will see
beneath the bustle of activity to the students as they become
immersed in their work. Not only do the students develop
problem-solving and thinking skills, they also learn to collaborate
and communicate orally and in writing. Most important, they
become motivated self-learners who carry their quest for learning
far beyond the classroom.

0–435–08796–7 / 1994 / Paper

History Workshop
Reconstructing the Past with Elementary Students
Karen L. Jorgensen
Foreword by Yetta Goodman

History Workshop is the first book to describe a process approach
to history teaching that builds on children's natural curiosity about
the past. Karen Jorgensen bases her work on the sociolinguistic
premise that history learning is a language-thinking process in
which children create historical meaning as they interact with
others. In her book, she describes how children understand
history. She also explains how she adapts the writing workshop
approach to a studio environment that encourages students to
discover and rethink theories as they talk, read, write, and draw.

0–435–08900–5 / 1993 / Paper

The Story of Ourselves
Teaching History Through Children's Literature
Edited by Michael O. Tunnell and Richard Ammon

In *The Story of Ourselves*, the contributors focus on the need for a stimulating history curriculum, with the application of children's trade book literature as an indispensable ingredient for such a curriculum. A collection of writings by trade book authors, as well as public school and college-level educators, the book offers support and instruction for teachers who decide to use literature in their history/social studies programs.

0–435–08725–8 / 1992 / Paper

These and other helpful resources are available through your local supplier or favorite bookstore.

Heinemann
361 Hanover Street
Portsmouth, NH 03801-3912
1-800-541-2086